Understanding

Lord of
the Flies

UNDERSTANDING GREAT LITERATURE

Andy Koopmans

LUCENT
BOOKS

THOMSON
™
GALE

San Diego • Detroit • New York • San Francisco • Cleveland
New Haven, Conn. • Waterville, Maine • London • Munich

On cover: Author William Golding is pictured at his home in 1983

To my teachers, for sharing with me their love of literature

LIBRARY OF CONGRESS CATALOGING-IN-PUBLICATION DATA

Koopmans, Andy.
   Lord of the flies / by Andy Koopmans.
      p. cm. — (Understanding great literature)
Includes bibliographical references and index.
Summary: Discusses *Lord of the Flies* by William Golding, including the author's life,
the book's historical background, its plot, characters, and theme. Literary analysis of
the novel is included.
ISBN 1-56006-786-1 (alk. paper)
   1. Golding, William, 1911– Lord of the flies—Juvenile literature.
   2. Survival after airplane accidents, shipwrecks, etc., in literature—Juvenile literature.
   3. Boys in literature—Juvenile literature. I. Title. II. Series.
PR6013.O35L6345 2003
823'.914—dc21

                                             2003000407

Printed in the United States of America

Contents

FOREWORD

"Except for a living man, there is nothing more wonderful than a book!" wrote the widely respected nineteenth-century teacher and writer Charles Kingsley. A book, he continued, "is a message to us from human souls we never saw. And yet these [books] arouse us, terrify us, teach us, comfort us, open our hearts to us as brothers." There are many different kinds of books, of course; and Kingsley was referring mainly to those containing literature—novels, plays, short stories, poems, and so on. In particular, he had in mind those works of literature that were and remain widely popular with readers of all ages and from many walks of life.

Such popularity might be based on one or several factors. On the one hand, a book might be read and studied by people in generation after generation because it is a literary classic, with characters and themes of universal relevance and appeal. Homer's epic poems, the *Iliad* and the *Odyssey*, Chaucer's *Canterbury Tales*, Shakespeare's *Hamlet* and *Romeo and Juliet*, and Dickens's *A Christmas Carol* fall into this category. Some popular books, on the other hand, are more controversial. Mark Twain's *Huckleberry Finn* and J.D. Salinger's *The Catcher in the Rye*, for instance, have their legions of devoted fans who see them as great literature; while others view them as less than worthy because of their racial depictions, profanity, or other factors.

Still another category of popular literature includes realistic modern fiction, including novels such as Robert Cormier's *I Am the Cheese* and S.E. Hinton's *The Outsiders*. Their keen social insights and sharp character portrayals have consistently reached out to and captured the imaginations of many teenagers and young adults; and for this reason they are often assigned and studied in schools.

These and other similar works have become the "old standards" of the literary scene. They are the ones that people most often read, discuss, and study; and each has, by virtue of its content, critical success, or just plain longevity, earned the right to be the subject of a book examining its content. (Some, of course, like the *Iliad* and *Hamlet*, have been the subjects of numerous books already; but their literary stature is so lofty that there can never be too many books about them!) For millions of readers and students in one generation after another, each of these works becomes, in a sense, an adventure in appreciation, enjoyment, and learning.

The main purpose of Lucent's Understanding Great Literature series is to aid the reader in that ongoing literary adventure. Each volume in the series focuses on a single literary work that a majority of critics and teachers view as a classic and/or that is widely studied and discussed in schools. A typical volume first tells why the work in question is important. Then follow detailed overviews of the author's life, the work's historical background, its plot, its characters, and its themes. Numerous quotes from the work, as well as from critics and other experts, are interspersed throughout and carefully documented with footnotes for those who wish to pursue further research. Also included is a list of ideas for essays and other student projects relating to the work, an appendix of literary criticisms and analyses by noted scholars, and a comprehensive annotated bibliography.

The great nineteenth-century American poet Henry David Thoreau once quipped: "Read the best books first, or you may not have a chance to read them at all." For those who are reading or about to read the "best books" in the literary canon, the comprehensive, thorough, and thoughtful volumes of the Understanding Great Literature series are indispensable guides and sources of enrichment.

The Lesson

William Golding's first novel, *Lord of the Flies*, was the most popular of his works and remained so throughout his distinguished career as a writer. *Lord of the Flies* had gained its enormous popularity in the late 1950s and early 1960s at college campuses in the United States and became required reading at most of them. Thus, questions about the book persisted for decades after the book's publication. Golding was repeatedly called upon by correspondence to explain things about the novel, and often these letters came from panicked students nearing exams. On a lecture tour of the United States in 1962, Golding delivered a lecture at numerous American universities, addressing many of the questions he had received about the novel over the years. However, in the lecture (published as "A Fable" in *The Hot Gates and Other Occasional Pieces*) Golding also lamented that, although he had retired from teaching, *Lord of the Flies* made him, permanently, a schoolmaster. He wrote:

> It is in some ways a melancholy thought that I have become a school textbook before I am properly dead and buried. To go on being a schoolmaster so that I should have time to write novels was a tactic I employed in the struggle of life. But life, clever life, has got back at me. My first novel ensured that I should be treated for the rest of my days as a schoolmaster.[1]

It was no mistake that the novel became such a popular teaching tool. Golding carefully planned and wrote the novel as a fable, a literary form which, by its design, is intended to teach a moral lesson to readers. Golding's moral lesson came from the years he spent serving in the Royal Navy during World War II. During these years, he saw horrors of war that profoundly affected him. He wrote:

> I had discovered what one man could do to another. . . . I am thinking of the vileness beyond all words that went on, year after year, in the totalitarian states. . . . There were things done during that period from which I still have to avert my mind lest I should be physically sick. . . . They were done, skillfully, coldly, by educated men, doctors, lawyers, by men with a tradition of civilization behind them, to beings of their own kind.[2]

Golding arrived at the conclusion that humanity inherently possessed potential for immorality and evil that was a danger to the world. "Man is a fallen being," he wrote. "He is gripped by original sin. His nature is sinful and his state perilous."[3] As a writer and a teacher, he set out to write *Lord of the Flies* to call people's attention to this condition. He admired the form of the fable for its "method of penetrating the truth,"[4] and he felt it would allow him to teach his moral lesson about the depravity of humanity to his readers.

Traditionally, fables are short stories, usually involving animals that talk and act like people. The stories often satirize human character flaws or traits to teach a lesson or convey a moral about humanity. The first fables still in existence date back to ancient India and to the stories of Aesop. Aesop was a sixth-century-B.C. Grecian slave whose fables, such as "The Hare and the Tortoise" and "The Fox Without a Tail," are still popularly read in cultures all over the world.

Over time, while fables became less popular than they were in ancient and medieval times, the form remained. Writers

After witnessing acts of brutality in World War II, author William Golding concluded that humanity is innately evil and immoral.

adapted and changed the form in various ways. For instance, some writers have adapted the short form into novel-length works, and others have used human characters rather than animals. Some popular fables include novels such as John Bunyan's seventeenth-century Christian allegory *Pilgrim's Progress*, eighteenth-century satirist Jonathan Swift's novel *Gulliver's Travels* (which many critics argue greatly influenced Golding), and twentieth-century British novelist George Orwell's *Animal Farm* (written in 1946).

In writing the novel as a fable, Golding broke from the central tradition of novels of social manners that had been predominant in English fiction since the eighteenth century. As scholar Khandkar Rezaur Rahman wrote, Golding's novel stood apart because it focused on the fundamental and eternal qualities of humanity, which was unusual in traditional and contemporary English literature:

> The English novel is not traditionally concerned with expression of metaphysical ideas; its strength, as it appears, lies in its presentation of social life rather than the metaphysics of human behaviour. . . . Golding stands apart from the main tradition because he is not interested in the social milieu as many of his contemporaries are.[5]

Golding's unusual use of realistic elements and fable-like symbolism in combination made the novel unique. The two strategies seemed to work against each other by their nature. However, as critics Bernard S. Oldsey and Stanley Weintraub wrote, it was this union of the real and the fabulous that made the novel so strong: "Paradoxically—yet artistically—this very tension between realistic novel and allegorical fable imparts to *Lord of the Flies* some of its unique power."[6]

Even in the late 1990s and in recent years, *Lord of the Flies* remains one of the most taught novels in literature. It endures because Golding's fable still teaches a lesson of value. As author Herbert N. Foerstel writes, the book remains important because it "encourages readers to confront the major question haunting the world today: How can civilized society elude the barbarism that pursues it?"[7]

CHAPTER ONE

The Life of William Golding

W illiam Golding's work is characterized by his underlying pessimism regarding the nature of humanity.
Like his writing success, this pessimism developed
relatively late in his life. Under the influence of his rationalist,
socialist parents, Golding was raised to believe in the per-
fectibility of humanity through science and reason. However,
the philosophy of his parents was no longer viable to Golding
as he grew older, particularly after he witnessed the horrors of
World War II during his service in the Royal Navy. When he
returned from the war, Golding explored his notions about
the innate evil of humanity throughout his large body of work,
beginning with his first published novel, *Lord of the Flies*.

Although he did not become an established author until
he was in his forties, Golding's imagination, as well as his love
of words and desire to write, developed early. "I began to
write when I was seven," he said, "and I have been writing off
and on ever since."[8] Golding took a circuitous route to his
avocation and profession as a full-time writer, serving as a
sailor during World War II and as a schoolteacher. First published as a poet while in college, Golding did not publish
again for twenty years, with *Lord of the Flies*. However, from

then to the end of his life, Golding wrote a dozen novels, four novellas, three collections of essays, and a play, establishing himself as one of the most renowned and honored writers of the twentieth century.

Origins

William Gerald Golding was born September 19, 1911, the second child of Alec and Mildred A. Golding (née Curnoe), at his maternal grandmother's house in the town of Newquay, Cornwall, in southwestern England. Golding's parents, particularly his father, were a strong influence on him. Alec Golding was the son of a shoemaker from the town of Kingswood, near Bristol. Alec had met Mildred Curnoe in the early 1900s, and the couple married in December 1904, in Mildred's hometown of Truro, Cornwall. They had their first child, a son named Joseph, in 1905. William followed six years later. The last member to join the Golding's immediate family was Eileen, a niece the Goldings adopted after the death of her parents in the 1930s, whom Golding as an adult referred to as his sister.

The Golding family lived in the town of Marlborough, Wiltshire, where Alec Golding was science master at Marlborough Grammar School, a government-funded secondary school similar to an American public high school. All the Golding children attended Marlborough Grammar School during their lives, and each in turn was instructed in science by their father both at home and at school.

Alec Golding was also a lifelong agnostic and rationalist. While Golding later said that his father did not scoff at religion, he had no use for it. Alec Golding firmly held the belief that reason and science were the best means of understanding the world, and he worked to instill this faith in rationalism in his children.

Golding loved his father, and particularly admired his vast knowledge and abilities. Golding wrote:

He could carve a mantelpiece or a jewel box, explain calculus and the ablative absolute [a noun or pronoun form in Latin]. He wrote a textbook of geography, of physics, of chemistry, of botany, and zoology, devised a course in astronavigation, played the violin, the cello, viola, piano, flute. He painted expertly, knew so much about flowers he denied me the simple pleasure of looking anything up for myself.[9]

Alec and Mildred Golding were socialists and very politically active. Alec Golding was an activist for the British Labour Party, and he and Mildred both were participants in political demonstrations in favor of women's suffrage (right to vote) in the early 1900s. According to Golding, during these demonstrations his parents withstood having rotten tomatoes thrown at them by those in the crowd who disagreed with the cause. Golding admired his parents' activism and, like them, would become a lifelong socialist, interested in the pursuit of a society where equality and fair treatment for all people would be possible.

A Wild Child

Starting school as a child when he was about six, Golding had a difficult time adjusting to being around other children. Before attending school, he had spent most of his time around his family or in the company of his nurse, Lily, and not with other children. "I was difficult," he admitted. "No one had suggested, before this time, that anything mattered outside myself. I was used to being adored."[10]

In response to the new environment at school, he began getting into fights. He was robust and enjoyed fighting so much that he soon ran out of opponents. He remembered not understanding why other children did not enjoy being his victims. He wrote:

Fighting proved to be just as delightful as I thought. I was chunky and zestful and enjoyed hurting people.

I exulted in victory, in the complete subjugation of my adversary, and thought that they should enjoy it too— or at least be glad to suffer for my sake.[11]

At school, Golding also noticed the violence of other children toward one another. According to Golding's daughter Judith Carver, the violence he witnessed and participated in at school was possibly an important foundation for his writing. She wrote, "The effect . . . on an impressionable ten-year-old may have had important results. [The violence of] the school playground may have lain dormant for years until some later experience pushed it to the surface as *Lord of the Flies*."[12]

Passion for Words

During these difficult first years of school, Golding developed an almost obsessive fascination with words. "I had a passion for words in themselves, and collected them like stamps or birds' eggs,"[13] he wrote. Golding spent much of his early school days ignoring his other lessons while making lists of words, enjoying the sound and look of them. He remembered:

> I was supposed to be writing out my [math] tables, or even dividing four oranges between two poor boys, [but] I was more likely to be scrawling a list of words. . . . While I was supposed to be learning my Collect [prayer], I was likely to be chanting inside my head a list of delightful words which I had picked up God knows where.[14]

Golding read voraciously, enjoying poetry, adventure novels, classics, and other genres. Like many children, he was particularly interested in adventure novels such as *Robinson Crusoe, Treasure Island,* and *Gulliver's Travels*. Golding also appreciated the work of turn-of-the-twentieth-century American humorist Mark Twain. According to Golding's daughter, Twain's attitudes and humor influenced Golding. She wrote: "[He liked] the Mark Twain of *Roughing It* and

The irreverent writing style of Mark Twain reinforced Golding's natural skepticism.

Innocents Abroad. He swallowed these. . . . The humour of these books and their irreverence towards many accepted things encouraged his own scepticism."[15]

Reading fed Golding's already vivid and powerful imagination. He recalled that the strength of his imagination was such that he often had trouble discerning reality from fantasy. "I imagined things so strongly that I saw them," he said. "I have a vivid imagination, and made no distinction between what was true and what wasn't."[16]

Writing

Golding's own writing grew out of his imagination, his passion for words and language, and his immersion in books. Writing became his natural response to people or things in which he became interested. At seven, he attempted a play on Egypt as well as imitations in poetry of his favorite Victorian-era poet, Alfred Tennyson.

At twelve years old, his socialist upbringing led him to begin writing his first novel, which he planned as a twelve-volume work. As an adult, he remembered the first line: "I was born in the Duchy of Cornwall on the eleventh of October, 1792, of rich but honest parents."[17] However, Golding quit the novel after the first few pages because he felt that he could not maintain the high standard set by the first line.

Golding persisted with writing throughout his childhood and adolescence. However, from early on he did not see it as a future profession. His father had other plans for him.

Breaking Away

Despite his passion for words and writing, Golding spent his secondary school years at Marlborough Grammar School preparing to follow his father's wishes to study science in college to become a biologist. Golding's admiration for his father was so great that he had grown up trying to model himself after the man even when he was quite different from his father. He later said:

> I'd been in [my father's] shadow, particularly, I suppose, philosophically, in that he had made of himself a . . . rationalist . . . and because he was who he was, I took this [on]; and for a long time I suppose I half convinced myself I was a rationalist, atheist, and so on. Whereas I don't think I was instinctively any of these things at all.[18]

In 1930 Golding enrolled as a science major at Brasenose College at Oxford, but soon decided that he had made a mistake. He wanted to study English literature, but he delayed switching majors until his third year because, he said, he knew "it would hurt my father so much."[19] When he finally did make the change, it was a happy one.

As a precocious seven-year-old, Golding developed an interest in the works of poet Alfred Tennyson (pictured).

A Turning Point

Several biographers emphasize the shift in Golding's studies as a significant turning point in his career and his life. Raised to be a rationalist and a scientist by his father, Golding believed that literature and the humanities were better able to help him understand the world than science. In an essay he wrote years later, he said: "'Science' is not qualified to answer [the questions of life] with its measurements and analysis. They can be answered only by the methods of philosophy and art."[20]

From college onward, the inability of science to answer important questions about humanity and the universe became an important theme in Golding's writing. He began exploring ideas about religion and writing about the absurdity of the purely rational world. In his first published work, a thirty-four-page book of poems published in 1937 by Macmillan as part of its Contemporary Poets series, Golding wrote poems that openly challenged scientific and rationalist values. For example, one poem, entitled "Mr. Pope," satirizes the eighteenth-century scientist and philosopher Alexander Pope. Golding portrayed Pope as a man dissatisfied with the natural chaos of the stars, wishing to impose order on them and make them "stand in rows all trim and neat."[21]

Finding His Place

Critics gave little attention to Golding's *Poems*, and Macmillan did not invite him to contribute more writing. Despite the disappointment, Golding was interested in pursuing his writing, and, after he graduated from Brasenose College at Oxford in 1934 with a degree in English literature, he moved to London to write. He spent the year writing poetry and plays, as well as producing and acting in small, amateur theater companies.

Deciding that he could not make a living as a writer alone, in 1935 he took a job teaching at a school called Michael Hall in Streatham, South London. However, he left the school in the summer of 1937, deciding to return to Oxford to get his teaching diploma. He completed the degree a year later, at age twenty-seven, and moved to Maidstone, Kent, to teach at Maidstone Grammar School. There he met Mabel Ann Brookfield, called Ann, a twenty-six-year-old woman, later described by her daughter as "very clever, extremely pretty, and very active in politics and drama."[22] Golding and Brookfield became engaged and then married in September 1939, just a few weeks after the beginning of World War II.

In April 1940 the Goldings moved to a cottage in the village of Bowerchalke, outside of Salisbury, Wiltshire, where Golding took a teaching position at Bishop Wordsworth Grammar School. Although he could have taken a position at a more prestigious private school, as a socialist, Golding took the job at Bishop Wordsworth because it was a publicly funded school that aimed to increase access to education for poorer people. He took up the post, teaching English and Greek literature in translation.

In October 1940 Ann Golding gave birth to the couple's first child, whom they named David. Two months later Golding took leave from his teaching position to enlist in the Royal Navy for service in World War II.

Defining Moment

Golding served in the Royal Navy for four years. He recalled his initial respect and awe about the navy, writing, "I came to admire the navy as a structure, very much indeed. . . . I was probably uncritical of [the navy] for a time, I think. . . . It was very impressive."[23] Golding enlisted as an ordinary seaman but soon afterward took the officer's exam. Because of his science training, he did so well on the exam that he was made an officer and sent to a secret research center, where he worked under British prime minister Winston Churchill's scientific adviser. However, soon after he was assigned, he was injured while working with explosives and spent some weeks recovering in the hospital.

Upon his release from the hospital, he asked for reassignment at sea, saying it would be more peaceful than working at the research center. He attended a training program in Scotland to operate a minesweeping vessel, but by the time his training was over, the navy had decided that minesweepers were no longer necessary. Golding, then a lieutenant, was instead given command of his own ship, a rocket-firing vessel. Under his command the ship took part in the sinking of the famous German warship *Bismarck* on May 27, 1941. He also commanded the ship during its participation in the D day Allied invasion in June 1944, and during Operation Infatuate, the amphibious invasion of the Dutch island of Walcheren.

Golding was a successful sailor and won a reputation as a daredevil and for loving intense combat. However, this reputation was a misunderstanding. In fact, he disliked combat. Critic E.L. Epstein writes, "At moments of stress in the middle of action, his facial muscles would contract violently, producing a broad ghastly grin, which was interpreted by his men as pure delight of combat."[24]

The negative impact of what Golding saw during service profoundly affected him. His daughter Judith Carver writes, "His war years coloured the rest of his life."[25] According to Golding, during the war he lost his naive idealism and first realized man's tremendous capacity for evil.

In his disgust for the violence and inhumanity he saw during his service, Golding turned to Greek literature to escape. He spent much of his free time teaching himself Greek so that he could read his favorite authors in their original language. "Greek is the love affair of my life,"[26] he later said. The solace he found in the literature helped keep him sane during the war.

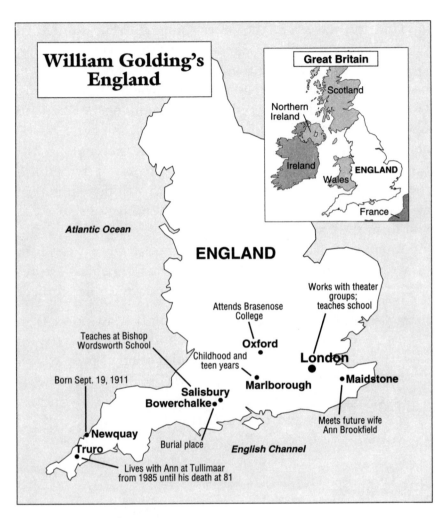

William Golding's England

Great Britain

Scotland

Northern Ireland

Ireland

ENGLAND

Wales

France

Atlantic Ocean

ENGLAND

Works with theater groups; teaches school

Attends Brasenose College

Teaches at Bishop Wordsworth School

Oxford

Childhood and teen years

London

Born Sept. 19, 1911

Marlborough

•Maidstone

Salisbury
Bowerchalke•

Meets future wife Ann Brookfield

•Newquay

Truro

Burial place

English Channel

Lives with Ann at Tullimaar from 1985 until his death at 81

Reluctant Schoolmaster

When Golding returned from the war in late 1944, he went back to work at his job at Bishop Wordsworth Grammar School in Salisbury to teach English and philosophy. Golding had no great love for teaching but saw it as a means of support for himself and his family (which had increased in number by one with the birth of daughter Judith in July 1945). "I wasn't teaching because I wanted to teach," he said. "I was teaching because it was a way of earning enough money to keep myself alive while I moved towards other things."[27]

High on the list of the other things Golding wanted to pursue was his writing. In the years following the war, Golding made several attempts at writing and publishing novels while teaching at Bishop Wordsworth. In his writing Golding explored what would become enduring themes in his work: the struggle of good and evil and the clash between science and humanism. He completed three never-published novels. In frustration from trying unsuccessfully to publish the work, he wrote, "This obsession with writing is pointless as alcoholism and there's no Authors Anonymous to wean you from the typewriter."[28]

After much frustration, Golding decided to take a risk in his writing. Instead of imitating the style or strategies of other writers, he decided to write a book in a new way. He recalled:

> I was always thinking to myself from the last novel I had read. Oh, so that's how you should write a novel, so my novels were splendid examples of other people's work. And it was only when I was so far from succeeding that I thought, well, to hell with it, I'll write my own book and devil take the hindmost. Then I wrote *Lord of the Flies.*[29]

Success

At first *Lord of the Flies* seemed destined to remain unpublished like Golding's previous novels. Over twenty publishers turned Golding down. However, the manuscript was finally accepted by London publisher Faber and Faber and published in 1954. While the novel took some time to gain attention, its publication led him to write and publish three other novels—*The Inheritors, Pincher Martin,* and *Free Fall*—and a play, *The Brass Butterfly,* in quick succession during the remainder of the 1950s. In the early 1960s *Lord of the Flies* became a best-seller, earning Golding enough money to survive on his writing alone. He retired from Bishop Wordsworth in 1961.

Golding took advantage of his new status and freedom as a successful writer to pursue his hobbies, which included sailing. He bought a boat and sailed the English Channel, the Dutch coast, and the North and Baltic seas.

Ups and Downs

Critical response to Golding's early works was positive at first. Critical reaction for his second and third novels, *The Inheritors* (1955) and *Pincher Martin* (1956), was generally favorable; however, many critics disliked his fourth novel, *Free Fall* (1959), and even more negative criticism appeared in response to his fifth novel, *The Spire* (1964), a story about the construction of the enormous cathedral spire in Salisbury. Many critics complained that the novel was unbelievable because Golding had not bothered to research the technical reality of a spire construction. Golding later admitted that he had intentionally set aside such research in favor of his imagination. According to some critics, *The Spire* marked a significant point in Golding's writing career. Critic Jonathan W. Doering writes, "It is from this point in time that Golding entered a period of critical eclipse, which lasted for the rest of the 1960s and much of the 1970s."[30]

Golding's output of writing was relatively sparse over the next fifteen years, and critical response to his work was lukewarm. After *The Spire,* Golding published *The Hot Gates and Other Occasional Pieces* (1965), a collection of nonfiction essays—among them the autobiographical "Billy the Kid" and "The Ladder and the Tree"—and one other novel, *The Pyramid* (1967), which many criticized as being a collection of short stories rather than an actual novel. When Golding published another collection of short work, *The Scorpion God,* in 1971, some critics questioned whether Golding was still a novelist at all and wondered whether his short career was over. Critic Jonathan W. Doering writes, "At least one scholarly journal ran a summary bibliography of Golding's oeuvre [body of work] during this time: some voices seemed to be whispering that not only was Golding erratic, but that he had already produced his life's work."[31]

Some critics defended Golding against the skepticism about his work and career. In 1965 critics Bernard S. Oldsey and Stanley Weintraub wrote, "He has become one of the most significant novelists writing in English, and—an irony, considering the intellectual demands he places upon his readers—one of the most read."[32]

Struggle

Golding struggled with his writing in the late 1960s and early 1970s. However, those who knew him said that the critical response to his work had not much affected him. His daughter wrote, "He felt, not that it [critical opinion] didn't matter, but that it wasn't his job."[33]

Golding continued to work during the years when he was not regularly publishing. In 1971 he began keeping a record of his dreams to help revive his writing. And throughout the 1970s he wrote two novels concurrently, *The Darkness Visible* and *Rites of Passage,* which he published in 1979 and 1980, respectively. Critics received *The Darkness Visible* and *Rites of Passage* with almost unanimous praise and acclaim. Many critics said that Golding's newer novels were nearly as good as his earliest work.

Golding also traveled a good deal during this period. Among the trips he made was to Egypt in 1976, a place of abiding interest since his childhood. The trip was a disappointment due to illness and difficulties, however. He would return again in the mid-1980s, enjoying it more and publishing *An Egyptian Journal* in 1984, telling of his trip sailing down the Nile.

Honors

Golding achieved some of the world's most prestigious writing honors during the later years of his career. In 1980 he won Great Britain's most prestigious literary award, the Booker Prize, for *Rites of Passage*, and in 1988 he was knighted Sir William Golding by Queen Elizabeth II. But the most prestigious award he received was the Nobel Prize for literature in 1983, in response to his well-received book of essays, *Moving Target*. The title of the book referred to Golding himself, in reference to his ever-changing style and strategies in his writing.

While Golding felt honored by the Nobel Prize, he did not enjoy the increased notoriety he received. Always a private man who did not enjoy celebrity as much as the work of being a writer, he felt an irritation with critics, academics, and fans.

Golding poses with his wife Ann outside their home in 1983, the year in which he won the Nobel Prize for literature.

Golding was so annoyed with his notoriety that he wrote a novel about it. *The Paper Men,* published in 1984, is about a novelist who is ruthlessly pursued by an American scholar. Journalist James Wood wrote that the novel was a warning: "The book functions as a kind of open letter of complaint: read this and stay away."[34]

Last Years

Golding spent the last years of his life mostly out of the public eye, with the exception of some interviews. He continued writing, and in the mid-to-late 1980s he published two more novels, *Close Quarters* and *The Fire Down Below.* From 1985 onward, Golding and his wife lived in a remote Georgian house called Tullimaar in Truro, Cornwall, near where his parents had married in 1904.

In addition to his writing, he continued to pursue his other interests, including being with his family (which grew to include three grandchildren), studying Greek, and playing the piano.

Golding died suddenly of a heart attack at home on June 19, 1993, at the age of eighty-one. He was buried in Bowerchalke in the churchyard next to the former vicarage where his wife and son had lived briefly after he had left for the navy.

His last novel, *The Double Tongue,* was in its third draft at the time of his death. It was published posthumously in 1995. In an essay eulogizing Golding, critic Robert McCrum wrote: "He'll be remembered as one of the great writers of the mid- to late-twentieth century, due to the power and imagination of his work, the luminousness of the prose."[35]

CHAPTER TWO

Historical Background of the Novel

W illiam Golding wrote *Lord of the Flies* in the early 1950s, during what many historians regard as a period of mixed turmoil, prosperity, and anxiety in the West. Critics note that the historic events surrounding the publication and reception of *Lord of the Flies* created an atmosphere in which reading audiences were able to understand the novel's darker themes and that the novel's eventual success had as much to do with its timing as with its literary strengths. The fluctuations of its popularity through the decades following its publication serve to support this theory.

Golding returned to Britain after his service in World War II. The country had sustained great physical and economic damage during the course of the war. Much of Britain had sustained heavy shelling during the Battle of Britain, and the war had cost the country an estimated 420,000 casualties at home and abroad, leaving a great loss of manpower for business and industry after the war.

Because of the economic slump following the war, Britain lost its leadership in world trade to the United States, whose industries and cities had been physically untouched by the war. Under the Labour government of Clement Attlee, Britain

Under Joseph Stalin, the Soviet Union seized control of several countries and placed them under Communist rule.

underwent great reform to alleviate the economic problems. Social services were extended to provide for people in need, and the British Labour government took large loans and aid from the United States to rebuild. Additionally, many of Britain's private industries were nationalized, including the Bank of England, the coal industry, electricity, tranportation, and medicine. However, the reform efforts made by the Labour government were unpopular, and the Labour Party eventually lost favor, being voted out of office in 1951.

The Soviet Threat

Following World War II, many Western leaders were concerned about the threat of communism spreading from the expanding Soviet Union into Western Europe, Asia, and potentially into the Americas. Although during the war the Soviet Union had fought with the Allied forces against the Axis powers of Germany, Italy, and Japan, in the years immediately following the war, the Soviet Union, under the leadership of Joseph Stalin, took control over several Eastern European countries formerly occupied by Nazi Germany, placing them under Communist rule. These countries included Poland, Czechoslovakia, and Eastern Germany, and this occupation created what British prime minister Winston Churchill called an Iron Curtain of communism.

Stalin considered capitalism the main enemy of communism and warned Western democracies that he intended to fight that enemy. Meanwhile, President Harry S. Truman began sending American military and economic aid to rebuild war-torn Western Europe and sanctioning aid to countries such as Greece that were threatened by Communist takeover.

Cold War and Atomic Anxiety

The threat of possible aggression between the West and the Iron Curtain countries escalated exponentially on September 23, 1949, when the Soviet Union successfully detonated its first atomic bomb. Until that time, the United States had been the only country with atomic weapons, and this advantage had given the West significant advantage and security. However, with the Russians a nuclear power, a period of ideological, economic, and military competition and conflict began between the United States and its allies and the Soviet Union. Both the United States and the Soviet Union began stockpiling nuclear weapons, and the threat of atomic warfare grew. While no state of combat existed between the United States and the Soviet Union, it marked the beginning of what historians call the Cold War, and it would last until 1989, when the Soviet Union's Communist government collapsed.

In Europe and in the United States, the Cold War era was characterized by widespread anxiety. As historian Diane Andrews Henningfield wrote:

> In the early 1950s, the world appeared to be divided into two camps: the so-called Free World of Western Europe and the United States, and the so-called Iron Curtain world of communist eastern Europe and the Soviet Union. At the time of the writing of *Lord of the Flies*, the world appeared to be teetering on the brink of total nuclear annihilation.[36]

Golding's Outlook

As a writer living in this era, Golding was susceptible to these anxieties. As critic Pat Rogers writes, "Golding is sunk as deep as his fellows in the morass of fifties uncertainty and panic."[37] Golding had been profoundly affected by his service in the Royal Navy during World War II. The violence he had witnessed dramatically changed his outlook on humanity. He had seen terrible deeds committed by both sides in the war and believed that all people, not just the Nazis, were morally diseased and capable of great evil. As critic Thomas R. Whissen writes, "When Golding saw the ecstasy on the faces of his fellow sailors in the North Atlantic as they returned fire on the enemy or launched an attack he felt the shock of recognition that the beast was within us all, just waiting to break through that fragile veneer we call civilization."[38]

The nuclear weapons buildup during the early years of the Cold War exacerbated Golding's concerns about the plight of humanity. When writing *Lord of the Flies*, he purposely set the novel in the context of a nuclear war. The boys in the book are schoolchildren being evacuated by air from Europe, which has been destroyed by atomic bombs.

Equally or more dangerous than weapons of mass destruction, however, was what Golding perceived as an attitude of self-satisfaction in his fellow Britons regarding their victory in the war. Proud of their hard-won triumph over Hitler's Nazi Germany, Golding saw that many people thought that the war had forever defeated evil. He wrote, "The outcome of the war had . . . lulled people into a false sense of security, as it was all too easy not to realize that evil could and would manifest itself again."[39]

The English saw evil in the fascism of the Nazis or the communism of the Russians but did not see their own capacity for it. Golding felt this attitude was misguided and dangerous. He wrote, "Men were putting the cart before the horse. They were looking at the system rather than the people. It seemed to me

These prisoners died trying to escape a building set on fire by the Nazis. Such hideous acts formed the basis for Golding's belief that humanity is inherently evil.

that man's capacity for greed, his innate cruelty and selfishness, was being hidden behind a kind of pair of political pants."[40] Unless people understood the universal potential for evil in humanity, he thought, tragedies and horrors such as those perpetrated during the war could arise again at any time.

Tracing the Connections of Evil

In the years following the war, Golding began writing novels to communicate his thesis of the innate evil of humanity and demonstrate how the diseased condition of man caused larger problems in the world. He wrote:

Man produces evil as a bee produces honey. . . . I believed that the condition of man was to be a morally diseased creation and that the best job I could do . . . was to trace the connection between his diseased nature and the international mess he gets himself into.[41]

As Golding set about to write what would become *Lord of the Flies,* he searched for a subject matter that he thought would demonstrate his thesis. He found it in the interactions among children that he remembered and witnessed. He wrote:

I looked round me for some convenient form in which [my] thesis might be worked out, and found it in the play of children. I was well situated for this, since at the time I was teaching them. Moreover, I am a son, brother, and father. I have lived for many years with small boys, and understand and know them with an awful precision.[42]

The inspiration for the novel took shape further after he read a boys' adventure story to his children one evening. Although he had loved this genre of stories when he was young, he was now frustrated with the unrealistic characters portrayed in the books. In the books the boys were unrelentingly virtuous and moral, demonstrating the Victorian idea of English superiority and morality. From his own experience with children, he knew that this was not how they acted. He was inspired to write his novel as an adventure tale, but he would populate the book with "real" boys and portray them as they would really act. He wrote:

I decided to take the literary convention of boys on an island, only make them real boys instead of paper cutouts with no life in them; and try to show how the shape of society they evolved would be conditioned by their diseased, their fallen nature.[43]

Revising *The Coral Island*

Golding chose to model his novel in part on *The Coral Island,* one of the most Victorian of the adventure novels. Written in 1857 by R.M. Ballantyne, the book had been a favorite of Golding's as a child. It tells the story of three British boys shipwrecked on an island in the South Pacific. The boys, Jack, aged eighteen, Ralph, the narrator, aged fifteen, and Peterkin Gay, aged thirteen, enjoy an idyllic life on the island, getting along well and surviving because of their English resourcefulness and luck. The only confrontation with evil or trouble comes from pirates and cannibals, whom the boys are able to conquer because of their Victorian moral and cultural superiority.

Golding decided to revise Ballantyne's novel by similarly stranding a group of boys on a deserted island but letting

In the 1990 film production of Lord of the Flies, *schoolboys land their raft on an island. Their behavior in the novel reflects Golding's pessimism about human nature.*

31

them act as he thought they really would. Golding borrowed the names of the main characters—Ralph, Jack, and Peterkin (who became Piggy)—and the setting and retold the story in a way he felt was more true to life and true to his vision of human nature. In Golding's version of the desert island story, the boys start out in the same kind of idyllic island as Ballantyne's characters in *The Coral Island*. However, the society established by the boys falls apart because they are human and victim to the defects of human nature, such as the fear of the beast and the bloodlust of Jack, Roger, and the other hunters. These internal human defects destroy their attempt at civilization and move them toward savagery and murder. Thus, Golding's novel was not only a revision but also a rebuttal of *The Coral Island* and the Victorian optimism it proclaimed.

While some critics argued that Golding's version is a pessimistic view of Ballantyne's book, Golding disagreed, saying his was the more accurate portrayal. "I think it is in fact a realistic view of the Ballantyne situation."[44]

Unpublishable

When Golding completed his novel, he titled it *Strangers from Within* and sent it out to publishers. He had previously written three novels that remained unpublished, and for a long while it seemed that his latest work would suffer the same fate. The book was rejected by twenty-one publishers. It was rejected for numerous reasons: Many publishers felt that the moral of the novel was too pessimistic and dark. Others did not know how to categorize the novel for marketing purposes.

Golding grew discouraged with the numerous rejections. However, he reread the novel and reconfirmed his commitment to it. He wrote: "I sat down and re-read it, and said to my wife, 'This is bloody good.' I also said to myself privately, 'One day this book will win me the Nobel prize.' And I was instantly appalled by my pride. But you see, I knew it was good."[45]

Finally, an editor named Charles Monteith at Faber and Faber publishers in London read the manuscript and saw its potential. He asked Golding to make some changes to the novel, including the removal of a military air battle that had originally appeared at the beginning. Golding made the changes and reconceived the title as *Lord of the Flies*, under which name Faber and Faber published the novel in 1954.

The Rise of a Best-Seller

Lord of the Flies did not make a large impact on the English public when it was released. Although the reviews were mostly positive, it did not receive much critical or popular attention, and within a year the book went out of print.

However, in 1955, an American edition was published by Coward-McCann publishers. The American edition became popular among university professors in the United States who introduced the book to their students. From there, popularity and critical attention grew steadily. This enthusiasm made its way back across the Atlantic to Britain and reawakened attention to Golding's novel.

While the pessimism of the book had scared away many publishers, the novel became increasingly popular *because* of this quality. World events, including the continuing Cold War, the Communist witch-hunts by the House Committee on Un-American Activities led by Senator Joseph McCarthy, the war in Korea, and the continued threat of nuclear war

The anxiety generated by Senator Joseph McCarthy's Communist witch-hunts sparked interest in Golding's novel.

had created an atmosphere of skepticism and anxiety in much of the Western world. Many readers found the pessimism of Golding's book appropriate. As critic Thomas R. Whissen wrote, "Readers who were attracted to this book in the fifties were at odds with a world that was sinking into complacency as a reaction to half a century of economic and political upheaval punctuated by wars of unprecedented horror."[46] This audience grew to the extent that by 1959, the book had sold sixty-five thousand copies.

Then, in 1961, Golding's audience grew even larger when the novel was rereleased in mass-market paperback. It became a best-seller in Britain and in the United States.

Lord of the Campus

Golding's novel sold particularly well on college campuses and in secondary schools, where teachers introduced it to their students as an alternative to the traditional English novel. The novel was a useful teaching tool. Its attributes as a fable encouraged interpretation, and it had many other qualities teachers looked for in a text. According to critic Bernard F. Dick, *Lord of the Flies* was

> well written and contain[ed] figurative language, ambivalence, symbolism that was natural [open to all readers] rather than private, foreshadowing, and empathetic characters; above all, it [was] teachable. . . . [Further], *Lord of the Flies* straddled the end of adolescence and the beginning of adulthood; it was, in short, the perfect book for an eighteen-year-old.[47]

The novel became so popular in the academic world that it eventually took the place of J.D. Salinger's 1951 novel, *Catcher in the Rye*. This was quite a feat, as *Catcher in the Rye* had been the most taught novel in many universities and schools for nearly ten years. Additionally, the usefulness of the novel transcended literature courses. It was assigned as required reading for political science majors as an example of utopia gone awry and, according to critic Bernard F. Dick, was given to Peace Corps volunteers to learn "the essential conflicts between man's individual well-being and the rules of society."[48]

Waning Influence

Lord of the Flies garnered great critical and popular attention through the early 1960s. The paperback edition of the novel sold several million copies, and the novel's success encouraged British director Peter Brook to make a film version in 1963 which was well received.

However, the popularity of *Lord of the Flies* shifted with the predominating atmosphere among youth, who were the core audience of the novel. In the mid-1960s, rising social awareness and political activism radically changed the outlook of many people, particularly among the young. The opposition to American involvement in an undeclared war in Vietnam, the rising feminist movement, and other social trends worked against the popularity of *Lord of the Flies*. The book's outlook became less popular, and it waned in favor of less pessimistic books. As Bernard F. Dick explains:

> A generation arose that was unwilling to accept evil as inevitable and human nature as intrinsically flawed. . . . [J.R.R. Tolkein's fantasy trilogy] *Lord of the Rings* replaced *Lord of the Flies*, [Herman] Hesse's *Steppenwolf* and [Ken] Kesey's *One Flew Over the Cuckoo's Nest*, with their unthreatening profundity, edged *Lord of the Flies* out of the introductory literature course. [The 1960s youth movement called] Woodstock nation rejected *Lord of the Flies* because "it no longer suits the temper of the times.[49]

Many critics and teachers who had once supported the book turned against it, calling it irrelevant to the times. In

1970 critic James R. Baker eulogized *Lord of the Flies* in his essay "Decline of the *Lord of the Flies*," saying, "The Golding vogue [trend] is over."[50]

Golding responded to the shift in favor with some bitterness. He felt that it was not a change in times but a decline in the level of sensibility and a public desire for feel-good books that were responsible for the novel's downward trend. He wrote:

> I dread to think of the next development—either complete neglect or [letters reading] "Dear Mr. Golding, my little Johnny is cutting his teeth on your *Lord of the Flies* and it give him a pain in his poor little tummy. Could you write another book that doesn't give poor little babies pains in their poor little tummies?[51]

Resurgence and Controversy

After about a decade of declining interest, *Lord of the Flies* returned to popularity in the 1980s. With the rise of leaders such as Margaret Thatcher in Britain and Ronald Reagan in the United States, 1950s-style conservatism became prevalent, and *Lord of the Flies*, which, because of its negative outlook on human nature was associated with conservatism by many, again fit the international mood.

Nevertheless, the critical themes of the novel bothered many people, among them parents and family groups such as the Eagle Forum, led by conservative activist Phyllis Schlafly. In the 1990s several family and religious groups attempted to have *Lord of the Flies* banned from public schools and libraries, charging that it was indecent and that Golding's pessimistic view of human nature and human society was inappropriate reading material for young students. While none of the attempts were successful, challenges of *Lord of the Flies* and other controversial novels persist into the present.

When conservative leaders like British prime minister Margaret Thatcher and U.S. president Ronald Reagan came to power in the 1980s, Lord of the Flies *saw a resurgence in popularity.*

An Abiding Novel

Despite its decline during the late 1960s and censorship challenges, *Lord of the Flies* remained an extremely popular novel. Golding remains best known for it out of the numerous other works he produced afterward, and critics overwhelmingly cite it as his greatest achievement. Since its publication, it has occasioned a casebook, numerous study guides, hundreds of articles, two films, and a play. The book has sold an estimated 15 million copies since its publication. Further, it remains among the top fifty books taught in American classrooms and the top one hundred books of the twentieth century in English recommended by the Modern Library Board's readers' poll.

CHAPTER THREE

The Plot

Lord of the Flies is divided into twelve chapters, vary-ing in length between ten and twenty-five pages long. The plot of the novel describes the characters' attempt to build a society on the island and that society's ultimate disintegration. Each chapter title reflects the main event in that portion of the book, and in this manner chap-ter titles act as a guide to the rise and fall of the boys' soci-ety on the island. For example, the first chapter, entitled "The Sound of the Shell," represents the sound of Ralph blowing the conch shell to call the boys to their first "civi-lized" assembly, and the last chapter title, "Cry of the Hunters," describes the sound of the boys as they hunt Ralph, their for-mer leader, through the jungle.

Chapter 1: The Sound of the Shell

As the novel opens, two young boys, Ralph and Piggy, meet each other in the jungle of a tropical island and make their way toward the beach. The boys' appearance is described, and they talk, revealing that they crash-landed on the island after an air battle during which their plane was hit.

On the beach, the boys discover a large conch shell, which Piggy tells Ralph how to use to call the rest of the boys on the island. Ralph blows the conch, and a large number of boys, ranging in age from five to twelve years old, comes out of the forest onto the beach in response. Among the boys is a choir-boy dressed in a heavy black cloak.

The choir leader introduces himself as Jack Merridew. Upon learning that there are no adults on the island, he says that the boys are going to have to figure out how to be rescued on their own. Ralph adds that they should elect a leader by vote. The boys elect Ralph because he is the one who has the conch and who called the boys together. Jack is upset by the decision, but Ralph assigns him control of the choir, which will hunt for the group.

Ralph, Jack, and another choirboy named Simon set out to explore the island to see if it is inhabited. They are happy and excited as they explore. They climb a mountain and see that they are on an island with a beach, a jungle, and a fort-like rock formation opposite the mountain on the other side.

Ralph (right) is elected leader of the stranded boys, while Jack (center) is given control of the choir, which will hunt for food.

The boys find a wild pig stuck in some of the jungle foliage, and Jack draws out his knife to stab the animal. However, he hesitates and the pig gets away. Ashamed, he declares that next time, he will not hesitate.

Chapter 2: Fire on the Mountain

Upon returning from the mountain, Ralph calls another assembly. He tells the other boys the island is uninhabited and that they will have to take care of themselves until they are rescued. He establishes his first rule as chief: to maintain order, only the person holding the conch shell is allowed to speak during assembly. Piggy takes the conch and lectures the boys. He says that the most important thing is being rescued because they may be there a long time. This upsets the boys, but Ralph says the island is good and they will have fun until they are rescued.

One of the youngest boys tells the group about a beast that he saw on the island. This scares the younger children, but the older boys dismiss it as a nightmare. Ralph changes the subject, talking about the good possibility of rescue. He says that they should build a signal fire on the top of the mountain for passing ships or planes to spot.

Excited, the boys run up the mountain. They collect wood, heaping a huge, disorganized pile. Using Piggy's glasses as a lens to focus the sunlight, they start a fire. As the fire grows, the boys continue piling more and more wood on the fire until it burns twenty feet high. However, the fire becomes too hot to emit smoke and dies out.

Piggy complains that the fire did no good, but Jack interrupts him. Piggy demands to be heard because he holds the conch, but Jack says the conch does not count on the mountain. The two argue but Jack wins because Piggy is afraid of him. Ralph takes the conch and declares the need for a watch on the mountain to keep the fire going and to watch for ships. Jack says the hunters will accept this responsibility.

Piggy lectures Ralph about the ineffectiveness of the first fire, breaking off when he sees that sparks have caught the surrounding forest on fire and it is burning out of control. Later, he points out that one of the boys is missing and probably burned to death in the fire. Ralph is ashamed but unwilling to admit that the boy is dead.

Chapter 3: Huts on the Beach

Weeks later, Jack is alone in the forest hunting a pig. After a long while of unsuccessful hunting, he leaves the forest and goes to the beach, where Ralph and Simon are attempting to construct huts.

Ralph complains to Jack that none of the boys but Simon are helping him. Jack says that Ralph is chief and should chastise them, but Ralph scoffs, saying it does no good. "They'd work for five minutes, then wander off or go hunting,"[52] he says. Annoyed, Jack argues that hunting is important. He tries to explain his growing need to hunt, "the compulsion to track down and kill that was swallowing him up."[53] However, Ralph complains there is still no meat despite all the hunting and that shelter and rescue are more important. He reminds Jack of the hunters' duty toward keeping the signal fire, and the boys argue—Jack mocking Ralph about his obsession with the fire, Ralph arguing that all Jack talks about is hunting pigs.

After Jack and Ralph leave for the bathing pool, Simon leaves the huts and walks into the forest. There, he helps some of the younger children, the "littluns," reach ripe fruit down from the trees, then moves on deeper into the forest. Once he is sure that he is alone, he finds a hiding place amid the bushes and foliage where he sits alone.

Chapter 4: Painted Faces and Long Hair

The chapter begins with a description of the daily cycle and routine on the island. Then, in the first scene, three littluns play

The boys gather around the slaughtered pig, eager to see its blood spilled.

on the beach until disturbed by two of the older boys, Roger and Maurice, who trample the littluns' sandcastle for fun.

Later, Jack calls Roger into the forest. Several hunters gather to paint each other's faces with colored clay and charcoal—like warriors. When they are done painting Jack, he looks at his reflection in a pool of water in a coconut shell and no longer recognizes himself. The boys then arm themselves and set off to hunt.

That afternoon, while Ralph and Piggy watch some of the boys swim in the lagoon, Ralph sees a ship on the horizon. He looks to the mountain and sees that the signal fire has gone out. He and the others rush to the mountaintop and find the fire dead, abandoned by the fire watchers. Ralph tries unsuccessfully to start the fire again and screams for the ship to come back, but it is no use.

Just then, the hunters return. Led by Jack, they are almost naked and painted. Sam and Eric, the fire tenders, carry a dead pig on a stake between them. The hunters chant as they approach: "Kill the pig. Cut her throat. Spill her blood."[54]

Ralph accuses Jack of his hunters' irresponsibility, and the two argue. Piggy joins the argument, and Jack hits him, breaking one of the lenses of his glasses. Ralph is so angry that Jack apologizes for letting the fire go out, but he refuses to apologize for hitting Piggy. Ralph remains angry and orders the hunters to relight the fire.

Later, the hunters hold a pig feast. When Jack refuses to give Piggy any of the meat, Simon gives some of his portion to Piggy, which angers Jack. Jack then leads the other hunters in an animated recounting of the hunt and soon the hunters begin dancing around the fire, singing, laughing, and stabbing the air with their spears.

Ralph watches the boys in silence. Finally, he stands and says he is calling a meeting and walks down the mountain alone.

Chapter 5: Beast from Water

At the meeting, Ralph lectures the boys about their failure to support his decisions as chief and chastises them for their failure to help construct the shelters or assist with the other chores such as keeping up the fire. He laments that order has broken down and that the littluns' fears of beasts must be addressed. "Things are breaking up," he says. "I don't understand why. We began well; we were happy. And then—. . . . Then people started getting frightened."[55]

Jack takes up the conch and berates the littluns for their fears of a beast. He says that he has been all over the island and has not seen any beast. Piggy speaks next, also agreeing that the littluns' fears are unscientific and irrational.

Nonetheless, a littlun named Phil says he saw a beast the night before, and another named Percival tells the group that he saw a beast come out of the sea. When Maurice acknowledges the possibility that sea monsters might exist, the boys grow more agitated and fearful.

The meeting becomes disorderly. Jack refuses to obey the rules of order and argues with Piggy over it. Then, Ralph and Jack end up arguing and shouting at each other. Finally, Jack curses and says that the hunters will hunt down the beast. He leaves the meeting, followed by most of the other boys.

Ralph, Piggy, and Simon remain behind. Ralph is depressed at the failure of the meeting, but Piggy and Simon encourage him. Piggy insists that he needs to remain chief or Jack will take over. He admits that he is scared of Jack.

They watch as the rest of the boys go chanting and dancing into their huts to bed down for the night. In the darkness, there is only the sound of one of the littluns crying.

Chapter 6: Beast from Air

The night of the meeting there is an air battle high above the island as the boys sleep. Unseen, the dead body of a pilot parachutes to the island and falls to the mountainside, where it gets stuck in some rocks. Still attached to the strings of the parachute, the figure moves almost as if alive whenever the wind blows and catches the fabric of the parachute.

In the predawn hours, the twins Sam and Eric sleep next to the fire. They wake to find the fire almost dead, and, while rekindling it, they see the parachutist and think it is the beast. They flee down the mountain to the huts and wake Ralph and Piggy to tell them. Too scared to leave their hut, the boys wait until dawn before coming out. Then, Ralph sends the twins to gather the others to assembly, afraid to blow the conch in case the beast might hear.

At the assembly, the twins describe the beast on the mountain, saying that when they ran from it, it chased them. The rest of the boys, especially the littluns, are terrified. However, Jack is excited. He wants to hunt the beast.

All of the older boys except Piggy agree to go on the hunt. Piggy remains with the littluns while the rest set off for the opposite end of the island near the rock formation, where they believe the beast is.

When they arrive at the rock formation, they find a castle-like edifice across a short stone bridge. The boys are afraid to venture further, but Ralph and Jack finally go together. While Jack thinks the place would make a good fort, Ralph does not like it.

Finding nothing, Ralph proclaims that the party must return to the mountain, to where the twins saw the beast. However, Jack and the other boys want to stay at the rock castle. Ralph overrules them and says that they must return to the mountain to relight the signal fire. The other boys reluctantly obey, Jack leading the way back.

The boys relax on the rock formation. Jack (left) proposes using the outcropping as a fort, but Ralph has a bad feeling about the place.

Chapter 7: Shadows and Tall Trees

On their way to the mountain, the hunting party stops to eat near the beach on the other side of the island. Ralph climbs down to the sand and sits alone, staring at the brutal, cold ocean. Ralph feels condemned to the island and believes he will never be rescued.

Simon joins Ralph on the beach and reassures Ralph. "You'll get back all right," he says, "I think so anyway."[56] Ralph tells Simon he is crazy, but his confidence returns and the two boys stand together smiling.

Later, Jack suggests another hunt and Ralph agrees, for the first time joining in with the others on a hunt. The boys find a wild boar in the jungle, and when it charges, Ralph throws his spear at it, hitting it in the snout but not killing it. The boar escapes, and although Ralph is exhilarated and proud of himself, Jack chastises his ineffective technique. To show him how to hunt, Jack orders the boys to make a ring with Robert pretending to be the pig. The boys chant and stab at Robert, becoming so excited by the play that they nearly kill him.

As darkness falls, Ralph decides that the hunting party should wait until morning to climb the mountain to find the beast. Jack accuses him of being a coward, successfully baiting Ralph into agreeing to climb up in the dark. However, Ralph insists that someone return to the camp to let Piggy know that they will return later than expected. Simon volunteers to take the message to Piggy and sets off alone.

When the hunting party finally reaches the mountain in the dark, Ralph stalls again, making excuses not to climb it. Jack mocks him, hurting Ralph's pride. Ralph asks, "Why do you hate me?"[57] but Jack does not respond. Instead, he starts up the mountain himself. Ralph and Roger follow him.

Ralph and Roger wait halfway up the mountain while Jack goes on to the top. Jack returns, claiming to have seen something, and the three creep to the top through the darkness on their hands and knees. In the moonlight, they see the pilot's body, "like a great ape was sitting asleep with its head between its knees."[58] As they watch, the wind catches the pilot's parachute, moving the body, and the boys flee in terror down the mountain, abandoning their spears.

Chapter 8: Gift for the Darkness

At camp the next morning, Ralph and Jack tell the others about the beast on the mountain. Piggy is disturbed. He cannot believe it. The boys discuss what to do, Jack suggesting that his hunters hunt the beast. However, Ralph rejects the idea, saying that the hunters are as scared as the rest of them. This makes Jack angry, and he grabs the conch, blowing it to call an assembly.

Jack announces to the boys that the beast is real. He also says that Ralph has insulted the bravery of the hunters and that Ralph is a coward because he would not go up the mountain first. He insists that the boys vote to throw Ralph out of office as chief, but none of the littluns will vote against Ralph. Angered and humiliated, Jack quits the tribe. "I'm not going to play any longer," he says. "Not with you."[59] He says that he is starting his own tribe and that anyone who wants to come and hunt and have fun with him can come. He runs off alone.

Later, Piggy and Ralph talk together, trying to decide what to do about the beast. Simon says that they should go up the mountain and confront it, but Ralph and Piggy do not want to. Ralph laments that they cannot have a fire on the mountaintop, which makes their hope of rescue almost impossible. He also feels that he cannot control the boys.

Piggy has the idea to move the signal fire down to the beach, which cheers Ralph. However, as they gather wood, Ralph notices that the older boys have left. Piggy says that they have gone off with Jack. Ralph becomes upset, but Piggy tries to convince him that they are better off without the other boys, particularly Jack. Then Ralph notices that Simon is also missing and wonders if he has gone to climb the mountain.

Covered in war paint, Jack's band of hunters stands armed with spears.

In the forest, Simon walks alone in the intense heat of the afternoon. He grows tired and thirsty and finds a hiding spot in the shade.

Meanwhile, far down the beach, Jack and his followers gather. Jack proclaims himself chief and says they will forget about the beast. He announces that they will hunt a pig. During the hunt, they find a sow nursing her piglets and cruelly slaughter it, thoroughly enjoying the kill. They cut off the sow's head and put it on a stick in the jungle as an offering for the beast.

From his hiding spot in the jungle, Simon witnesses the offering. When the others have gone, he approaches the head, and it seems to speak to him. It tells him to run away, to join the other boys, but Simon continues to look at the pig, the intense heat and thirst giving him a severe headache.

At the same time, Piggy and Ralph sit on the beach, talking and tending their fire. They try to figure out what to do now that there is only the two of them, Simon, Sam, Eric, and the littluns. Ralph is scared that they will never get rescued, and he does not understand what went wrong with their group. Piggy blames Jack.

Just then, Jack and two other boys covered in war paint break through the forest, screaming and shouting. They scare the littluns away. Ralph and the other older boys arm themselves in defense, but learn that Jack's group is only there to steal burning sticks for a fire. Jack tells them that his tribe is having a feast up the beach and that everyone is invited. After Jack's group leaves, Ralph and Piggy decide they will attend the feast to get some meat.

Meanwhile, Simon is still in the forest. The pig's head reveals itself as the Lord of the Flies and talks to him. The Lord of the Flies tells him that he is the reason for all their troubles on the island and that they cannot escape because he is part of all of them. Then, Simon faints.

Chapter 9: A View to a Death

A storm draws near the island that evening. Simon regains consciousness and decides to climb the mountain alone. He weakly crawls to the top, where he finds the dead pilot. He untangles the parachute from the rocks so that the body is no longer thrashed about by the wind. Then he decides he must tell the other boys as soon as possible. He staggers down the mountain toward Jack's camp.

Meanwhile, Ralph and Piggy arrive at the feast, where all the boys sit around Jack, who sits enthroned, "painted and garlanded . . . like an idol."[60] Jack gives Ralph and Piggy meat and, after everyone has eaten, invites all of those boys in attendance who have not already joined his tribe to do so. Most accept.

Ralph tries to reassert his power as chief. He points out that a storm is coming and they need his shelters, but Jack ignores him and orders his group of hunters to dance. All the boys join in, except Ralph and Piggy. The boys dance around the fire and pretend to hunt Roger, who plays the pig. They chant, "Kill the beast! Cut his throat! Spill his blood! Do him in!"[61] again and again. The boys become increasingly wild, and even Ralph and Piggy feel excited by the ritual. Suddenly, a black shape crawls out of the jungle, calling to the boys. It is Simon, but the boys do not recognize him or hear him. They leap on him and beat him with their spears. Despite his cries of pain, they continue until he is dead.

The storm breaks, dumping rain and blowing wind on the island, breaking up the melee. The boys run for shelter, leaving behind Simon's body, which washes into the sea. Overhead, caught by the wind, the parachutist's body glides into the lagoon and disappears.

Chapter 10: The Shell and the Glasses

The next morning, Ralph and Piggy meet near the fire. They discover that, other than Sam and Eric, they are alone. They try to talk about the events of the previous night but are ashamed and awkward. Piggy claims it was an accident and that they cannot think about it.

Meanwhile, Jack's tribe moves to the rock formation, now called Castle Rock. Jack announces that his hunters will hunt the next day and warns that strict security of the camp must be maintained while they are away in case the beast should try to enter. Jack says that the beast can never be killed and that he may come again. He also says that he and some other boys will go to steal fire from Ralph's tribe again.

After sunset, Ralph, Piggy, and the twins struggle to keep their small fire going. They are all depressed and guilt-ridden, too tired and listless to carry wood. They decide to let the fire go out for the night and go to their shelters.

Later, the boys awake to voices outside their huts. Suddenly Jack's group attacks. Ralph, Sam, and Eric fight back, confused and ineffective in the dark. Jack and his hunters retreat, but Ralph hears Piggy crying. Jack and the others have stolen his glasses.

Chapter 11: Castle Rock

At dawn the next day, Ralph, Piggy, and the twins sit next to the burned-out fire. Their situation seems hopeless. Piggy is almost blind without his glasses, and without the fire there is no chance of rescue. They decide they have to go to Castle Rock to talk Jack into returning Piggy's glasses. Piggy decides to take the conch with them as a symbol of authority and reason.

When they boys arrive at Castle Rock, guards challenge them from above. Ralph demands that they recognize him and blows the conch to call an assembly. Roger appears and tells them to leave, but Ralph refuses, saying that they are there to retrieve Piggy's specs.

Jack and a group of hunters appear on the path behind Ralph and the others, returning with a slaughtered pig. Ralph confronts Jack, demanding Piggy's specs. Jack tells them to leave, but when Ralph refuses, Jack orders two of his hunters to grab Sam and Eric and tie them up. Enraged, Ralph screams at Jack: "You're a beast and a swine and a bloody, bloody thief!"[62] He charges at Jack, and the two boys wrestle and fight.

Piggy interrupts, demanding that the others listen. Suddenly there is quiet, but as he begins to speak, Roger drops stones from above. The crowd of kids begins to clamor again. Piggy shouts above the noise, berating them for acting like savages. "Which is better," he shouts, "to have rules and agree, or to hunt and kill? . . . Which is better, law and rescue, or hunting and breaking things up?"[63]

The hunters get ready to attack Piggy and Ralph, but before that can happen Roger topples a large boulder from above. It crashes down on Piggy, killing him and shattering the conch.

Jack screams at Ralph, "See? See? That's what you'll get! I meant that!"[64] He throws his spear and it hits Ralph in the ribs. The other boys hurl their spears at Ralph, but he escapes into the jungle.

Chapter 12: Cry of the Hunters

Later Ralph sneaks into the jungle, trying to avoid running into any of Jack's hunters. He tries to convince himself that the boys will not come after him, but he realizes that Jack will never let him alone.

That evening, Ralph stumbles upon the pig's head in the jungle. He does not understand what it is, but he takes the sharpened stick on which the head is mounted as a weapon. Then, when darkness falls, he sneaks back to the camp at Castle Rock, where a feast is in progress. He finds Sam and Eric guarding the camp. Ralph pleads with them to come with him, but the twins tell him that Roger tortured them until they agreed to join the tribe. They tell Ralph that he has to leave, but they give him some food and warn him that the hunters are going to come after him in the morning.

Ralph spends the night not far from the camp, trying not to fall asleep. In the morning, he hears voices. Under torture, one of the twins has revealed Ralph's hiding place. Ralph also realizes Jack has set the area on fire to flush him out. He is forced out of his hiding place, but he manages to evade the hunters for a while. As they get closer to him, Ralph relies on his instincts to escape. He feels like an animal, a beast, running and searching for safety.

Finally, the hunters drive Ralph to the open beach, where he will have nowhere to hide. When he reaches the beach, he collapses. Then he looks up and sees a man dressed in a naval officer's uniform standing in front of him. Ralph is speechless, and the officer assumes that he has been playing a game. He explains that they saw the smoke from the fire and came to investigate.

Jack has lit a fire to flush out Ralph, forcing him to run to the beach. There, the boys find a naval officer and the "game" is over.

The hunters arrive on the beach and stop suddenly, falling silent when they see the officer. The officer is concerned when he sees the dress and look of the boys. He is shocked to find out that two of the boys have been killed.

Ralph realizes that they are rescued and that the horrors of the island are over. However, as he recalls the events of the past days, he starts crying. The officer is moved and embarrassed and turns away to look at his warship on the horizon.

CHAPTER FOUR

The Characters

The characters in *Lord of the Flies* are all English school-boys ranging in age from approximately five to twelve years old. The number of boys on the island is never made clear, but there are probably about fifteen to twenty boys total. The older boys are sometimes communally referred to as "the biguns" and the youngest children, who are five or six years of age, are called "the littluns."

In populating the island with so many boys, Golding created an array of diverse characters that serve various purposes in the novel. The main characters—Ralph, Jack, Piggy, and Simon—are all among the older boys. These four are described in the most detail, and each of these boys is made carefully distinctive from the others. For example, Ralph is blond, Jack redheaded, Simon dark haired and dark skinned, and Piggy fat, balding, and wearing glasses. Further, although readers learn less about secondary characters such as Sam, Eric, Roger, Maurice, Robert, and Bill, and even less about the rest of the boys, each of the characters on the island fulfills some service to the plot of the novel.

However, the descriptions of the characters in *Lord of the Flies* is different from those of many novels in that Golding omits information readers might normally expect to know about the boys. For instance, other than a few recollections of home that Ralph has in memory and dreams, readers learn almost nothing about the boys' lives before arriving on the island. Additionally, of the main characters, Golding gives only Jack Merridew a last name, and readers never learn Piggy's given name. Critics have argued that Golding purposefully made the boys' past and backgrounds vague to emphasize the universality of their experience. That is, who they are and where they came from is irrelevant because what happens to this pack of English schoolboys could happen to any human being, since innate human nature is the root cause of the trouble.

Bill

Bill is one of the older boys from the choir who becomes one of Jack's hunters. He is not given a physical description, but he is with Jack when Jack first paints his face, and he also takes part in the first successful hunt.

Like many of the hunters, Bill is violent. He enjoys hunting and slaps one of the littluns for crying. However, like Sam and Eric, Bill is afraid to hunt for meat in the jungle without Jack once the beast's existence has been confirmed.

Although he becomes loyal to Jack, Bill is not among the first boys to desert Ralph's tribe. Only after Jack invites Ralph's group to the feast does Bill defect. Bill becomes a guard at Castle Rock, and he searches for Ralph when he hides in the jungle around Castle Rock after Piggy's murder. At this point, Ralph notices that Bill, painted and dirty, no longer resembles the civilized English boy he once knew, and that, like most of the boys, Bill had become a savage. "But really, thought Ralph, this was not Bill. This was a savage whose image refused to blend with that ancient picture of a boy in shorts and shirt."[65]

Jack Merridew

The leader of the choirboys and eventual chief of the hunters, Jack Merridew is a tall, thin, bony boy with a full head of red hair and bright blue eyes. He is about twelve years old, perhaps a little older, and his face is "crumpled and freckled, and ugly without silliness."[66] From his first entrance in the novel, Jack appears menacing. Even his sinister costume of a heavy dark robe and cap calls up images of traditional villainy.

Jack loves power from the start, as is evident in the way he enjoys commanding the choir. He wishes to be called by

Golding reveals little about the former lives of the three main characters, Ralph, Piggy, and Jack. This device implies that each of us has the capacity for evil.

Jack is transformed from a civilized schoolboy into a bloodthirsty savage. His character is driven by a lust for power.

his surname rather than "Jack" and also believes that he is a natural leader, arguing that he should be chief when the boys hold their election. The loss of the election humiliates him.

Although Jack becomes a bloodthirsty, savage villain, he does not start this way. At first, much like the other boys, he is still conditioned by the society from which he came. For instance, in the first chapter, he is unable to kill the pig "because of the enormity of the knife descending and cutting into living flesh; because of the unbearable blood."[67] His gradual transformation into becoming the novel's villain occurs as he becomes obsessed with the hunt. He spends hours alone in the jungle. Golding writes, "The compulsion to track down and kill . . . was swallowing him up."[68] In a key transformative scene, Jack paints his face to prepare for what becomes the first successful hunt. When he is done, he does not even recognize himself. "He looked in astonishment, no longer at himself but an awesome stranger."[69]

As the novel progresses, Jack becomes increasingly violent, bloodthirsty, and power hungry. He is thrilled by his first successful kill. Each hunt and each kill make him more powerful in the group. He cares less about rescue. He wants to stay on the island because he is powerful there. By the end of the book, Jack has relinquished all of society's conditioning and has become a savage, acting in his own self-interest at the expense of anyone who disobeys or challenges him.

As Jack becomes engrossed in the pleasures of the hunt, he also becomes increasingly belligerent toward Ralph's leadership. From the beginning, Jack resents Ralph's leadership. He balks at the rules, especially the authority of the conch, which establishes the order of speaking at meetings. He challenges Ralph's decisions and actions, particularly when they infringe upon his pleasure. As the story develops, Jack gains the support of most of the group by preying on the boys' fears of the beast and desire for meat.

Jack's relationship with Ralph is one of the most important in the book. As their friendship turns to adversity, the breakdown in their relationship reflects the general descent of the group from civilization into savagery. As the plot progresses, Jack eventually becomes Ralph's main adversary and antagonist, turning the boys against him and then finally hunting his former friend down like an animal.

Maurice

One of the older boys and the largest in the choir next to Jack, Maurice is affable and generally good-natured at the start of the novel. He is described as "broad and grinning all the time."[70] He is athletic, a strong swimmer who is more at home in the water than any of the other boys. In the first chapters of the book he is as friendly toward Ralph as he is toward Jack and is diplomatic, twice defusing arguments or tense situations by changing the subject or clowning around to make everyone laugh.

Although he does not participate in the first hunt, which is responsible for the signal fire going out, Maurice allows himself to be led by Jack and Roger into acts of violence and cruelty. For instance, he follows along as sadistic Roger destroys the littluns' sandcastles on the beach. Unlike Roger, at this point Maurice retains enough of his social conditioning to run away in fear of punishment when one of the littluns begins crying from sand he has kicked into the child's eye. Golding writes, "In his other life Maurice had received chastisement for filling a younger [child's] eye with sand. Now, though there was no parent to let fall a heavy hand, Maurice still felt the unease of wrongdoing."[71]

Maurice frequently speaks at the meetings, and Ralph thinks of him as one of the active debaters when it comes to the topic of the beast. Maurice suggests that the beast from the water could be real, although, like the other older boys, he denies its existence. Like the rest of Jack's choirboys-turned-hunters, over time Maurice descends into savagery, shedding the social conditioning of home as the plot progresses. He participates in the hunts, including the brutal slaughter of the sow, after which Jack smears the sow's blood on Maurice's face in celebration of the violent kill. Maurice also sometimes plays the pig for the hunters' ritual reenactment, and he is one of the three boys who attack Ralph's encampment to steal Piggy's specs. Finally, he participates in the hunt through the jungle for Ralph at the end of the novel.

Piggy

Piggy is short and fat, as his nickname indicates, and he wears glasses and has asthma. His differences cast him as an outsider among the rest of the boys. Golding writes, "There had grown up tacitly among the biguns the opinion that Piggy was an outsider . . . by fat, and ass-mar [asthma], and specs, and a certain disinclination for manual labor."[72] Piggy is persistently teased and is a natural target for Jack's contempt and sadistic bullying. Even Ralph, who recognizes Piggy's value as a thinker, feels best when the group is teasing Piggy because he sees it as the natural order of things.

Piggy is the intellectual and most adultlike boy of the group. He is smart and is a firm believer in science. When the other boys begin to talk about the beast or ghosts, Piggy is quick to dispute their superstitions and fears as irrational. Piggy is also well versed in the rules and norms of the adult world for which he has such respect and regard. He has contempt for childish behavior, complaining that the boys act like a bunch of children, which of course they are. When trouble begins in the novel and the boys' fear begins to destroy their civilization, Piggy wishes for the intervention of adults.

Piggy's superior intelligence makes him the clearest choice for leader of the boys. For instance, although Ralph finds the conch—a symbol of society and order—Piggy knows that it can be used as a clarion to call the others. Nevertheless, his physical appearance and lack of social skills rule him out as chief. Instead, he becomes Ralph's adviser and proves to be his most loyal friend. Together, the two work to create a civil society on the island and to get the group rescued.

Along with the conch, Piggy's specs are associated with him and function as an important symbol in the novel. They represent his intelligence and his link to

In the 1990 film production, a forlorn Piggy sits alone. Highly intelligent, Piggy is bullied by the others.

science and the rational world, and his constant polishing of them shows his desire for clear-sightedness. The specs serve the important function of providing fire—and its promise of survival and rescue.

Piggy's specs are also associated with his vision, figuratively and literally. As the arbiter of civil society on the island, Piggy helps guide the group by figuratively seeing rationally and clearly. When Jack breaks one of the lenses after the first successful pig hunt, he loses some of his sight and society on the island is damaged. When Jack and the other boys steal his specs, Piggy is left blind, and the group is symbolically sightless. After this, the worst violence on the island takes place with Roger's deliberate killing of Piggy.

Piggy is killed because of his insistence on obedience to rules and order. His reverence for the conch symbolically represents his stubborn and misguided belief that civil society can defeat savagery and violence. His last words before Roger drops the boulder on him are "Which is better, law and rescue, or hunting and breaking things up?"[73]

Ralph

Ralph is the protagonist of the novel, described as fair-haired and a little over twelve years old. He has a boxer's build and eyes and a mouth that "proclaimed no devil."[74] The other boys elect him chief because he is tall and handsome and because he possesses the conch, an object that comes to symbolize order and society in the novel.

While Ralph admits to himself that he is not a thinker, he has common sense, a strong sense of morality, and knows right from wrong. Even so, Ralph is not morally infallible. He violates Piggy's trust by revealing the boy's dreaded nickname and joins in with the others in teasing him. He is also in part responsible for the fire on the mountain, which rages out of control, possibly killing the littlun with the birthmark. Further, as the novel progresses, the violence and bloodlust

Late in the story, Ralph (from the 1963 film) realizes that human nature has a dark core.

of the hunt tempt him. He takes great pride in hitting the boar with his spear, and when Robert pretends to be a pig for the other hunters, Ralph has to force himself to resist joining in the game because "the desire to squeeze and hurt [Robert] was over-mastering."[75] Finally, he and Piggy are both present on the fringe of the group when the hunters accidentally kill Simon, believing him to be the beast.

Nevertheless, aside from Piggy, Ralph is as close to a hero as readers get in the novel. He takes his responsibility as chief of the boys seriously, and he continually tries to make good decisions that are in the best interest of the entire group. He works to get the group rescued, requires the construction of huts on the beach, and is concerned for the welfare of the lit-tluns when it appears that the beast is a threat on the island.

Ralph is also the only one of the older boys to recognize Piggy's value to the group, turning to him for ideas and help in his duties as chief. The two boys relentlessly strive to create a democratic, civil society on the island and to keep order on the island. Ralph's main antagonist in these efforts is Jack, who challenges his authority, refuses to obey the rules, and leads the boys in a mutiny against Ralph for the promise of protection and meat.

At the beginning of the novel, Ralph is like the other boys on the island—naive, optimistic, carefree, and determined to enjoy the time without supervision on the island. However, as the novel progresses and tragedy follows tragedy, Ralph begins to understand the dark nature of humanity. At the end of the novel, he cries because of this knowledge. "Ralph wept for the end of innocence, the darkness of man's heart."[76]

Robert

Robert is among the older boys and one of Jack's hunters who, like Maurice, sometimes plays the role of the pig in the ritual hunting dances. During the ritual on the return from the hunt for the beast at Castle Rock, the hunters hurt Robert as they are carried away in a frenzy of violence.

Robert is a faithful and obedient henchman to Jack. He takes part in the first raid on Ralph's camp to steal fire and acts as watchman for the fort at Castle Rock. Robert also takes pleasure in violence and the pain of others. He laughs when Simon injures himself by running into a tree in the forest and becomes excited after the brutal slaughter of the sow. Further, Robert giddily reports to Roger about Jack's upcoming torture punishment of one of the littluns.

Roger

Described as a slight, furtive boy, Roger is one of the older boys. He is quiet, with "an inner intensity and avoidance and secrecy."[77] He is smaller and weaker than Jack, but eventually becomes more sadistic than any of the hunters, taking great pleasure in causing pain. He is also the only boy on the island to commit murder deliberately by dropping the boulder on Piggy.

Early in the book, when Roger knocks down the littluns' sandcastles and throws rocks at Henry, he is aware of the lingering social conditioning of his life before being stranded on the island. Golding writes, "Round the squatting child was the protection of parents and school and policemen and the law. Roger's arm was conditioned by a civilization that knew nothing of him and was in ruins."[78] However, as the novel progresses, Roger takes increasing pleasure in violence and destruction. During the killing of the sow, he is the most brutal, stabbing the pig repeatedly and cruelly inserting his spear into the pig's anus while it is still alive.

When Jack breaks off from Ralph's group, Roger is one of the first to leave after him, and, during the wild ritual dance the night of the storm, Roger actively participates in Simon's murder. Later, when Jack's tribe is settled at Castle Rock, Roger revels in the news of the littlun Wilfred's upcoming punishment. While Jack's desire for power arguably leads him to violence, Roger is excited by anarchy.

Roger becomes Jack's second in command and the tribe torturer and executioner, taking pleasure in his jobs. As he throws rocks down at Ralph, Piggy, and the twins as they approach Castle Rock, his excitement at the violence pulses in his body. Further, he experiences "delirious abandonment"[79] as he drops the boulder on Piggy, and he eagerly participates in the torture of Sam and Eric.

The symbol that comes to stand for Roger's sadistic nature is the stick sharpened at both ends. First used as a pike upon which to set the sacrifice of the pig's head, Sam and Eric tell Ralph as he hides from the others that "Roger sharpened a stick at both ends"[80] in preparation for the next day's hunt, indicating his intention of savagely decapitating Ralph after they have killed him.

Sam and Eric

Sam and Eric are twins, both blond, chunky, and vital boys whose resemblance to each other is shocking. Golding writes, "The eye was shocked and incredulous at such cheery duplication. They breathed together, they grinned together."[81] The twins, so interdependent that they must do everything

Golding uses a stake to symbolize Roger's (far left) sadistic character. Roger intends to impale Ralph's decapitated head on the end of the stake.

together, are eventually referred to simultaneously as "Sameneric." The twins are frequently assigned fire watch, although they prove irresponsible at the task. They abandon the fire and let it go out at the crucial moment a ship passes the island so that they can accompany Jack on the first successful hunt. They are also on watch the night that the parachutist drops in, and the two boys are asleep when it happens because one of them cannot stay awake while the other sleeps. "They could never manage to do things sensibly if that meant acting independently, and since staying awake all night was impossible, they had both gone to sleep."[82] Because of their irresponsibility, they mistake the parachutist for the beast, setting off the hysteria that causes the group's descent into fear and anarchy.

Besides Simon and Piggy, who are both killed, Sam and Eric are the last boys to remain loyal to Ralph, staying with him after the rest of the older boys leave with Jack and again after the littluns defect to Castle Rock. They help fight off the attack on the camp in which Jack's hunters steal Piggy's specs (although it turns out in the darkness and confusion that they were actually fighting each other). Finally, they accompany Ralph and Piggy on their journey to Castle Rock to retrieve Piggy's specs. There they are taken hostage by the hunters and tortured into joining Jack's tribe.

Even after their capture, Sam and Eric help Ralph by hiding him and giving him some food, but they finally betray Ralph. Under torture, one of the twins leads Jack and Roger to Ralph's hiding place in the jungle.

Simon

Simon is a "skinny, vivid little boy, with a glance coming up from under a hut of straight hair that hung down, black and coarse."[83] He is set apart from the other boys by his unusual behavior: He is shy, he often wanders off alone, and he has no fear of the jungle that terrifies most of the other boys.

Throughout the book, the other boys—even Piggy, who is also an outsider because of his appearance and intelligence—wonder about Simon's sanity, calling him queer, strange, and batty.

Simon possesses intuition and understanding that eludes the others, even Piggy. Simon is the first to suggest that the beast might actually be the creation of their own fears, but the other boys misunderstand and ignore him. Later, when Ralph sits brooding on the beach on the other side of the island about the hopelessness of being rescued, Simon tells him that he will be rescued. Whether this is an act of premonition or sympathetic kindness is unclear, but it does come true.

Simon's bravery also sets him apart. Unlike Jack or even Ralph, his bravery does not come from pride but from a sense of necessity. He is unafraid to go through the jungle alone to carry a message from the hunting party at Castle Rock to Piggy and the littluns. When Ralph and Piggy see no possibility for rescue because they can no longer build a fire on the mountain, he suggests going up to confront the beast.

Critics have compared Simon to Jesus Christ because of his altruism and kindness toward the other boys. He alone helps Ralph construct the huts, he reaches down ripe fruit from the trees for the littluns who are too short to reach, and he gives up his portion of meat to Piggy when Jack denies the boy at a feast. Additionally, like Jesus, Simon goes into the wilderness alone and has a revelation. An epileptic, though he does not know it, Simon watches as Jack and the hunters kill the sow and offer its head on a stick sharpened at both ends as a sacrifice to the beast.

Simon approaches the head and hallucinates, hears it speak to him. It reveals itself as the Lord of the Flies and tells him that it is the cause of all the boys' troubles on the island, that it is the evil that is within all of them. Simon goes to the mountain and sees the beast for what it really is, and then runs down to tell the others, only to be mistaken for the beast and killed by his friends. Again, like Jesus, he offers salvation and is slaughtered.

The Littluns

The littluns are the group of the youngest boys on the island. Aged five or six, they play a less significant role in the plot of the novel than the older boys. They spend most of the novel apart from the older boys and frequently do not seem to understand what is going on around them. The littluns that are given names in the novel are Phil, Percival Weyms Madison, Stanley, Wilfred, Harold, Henry, Walter, and Johnny.

In spite of their small role, the littluns are important in the novel for several reasons. They introduce fear of the beast through the night, causing annoyance and concern among the others. Further, they require the care and protection of the older boys. At first they choose Ralph as their natural protector because he is handsome and has the conch, but, as the fear of the beast becomes more powerful, they leave Ralph's tribe for Jack's because he can provide food and, they believe, protection.

Because the littluns are dependent upon the older boys for care, their presence also reveals aspects of the older boys' characters. Jack and the other hunters do not care about them or sympathize with their fears at first. Robert jokes that they hunt one of the littluns in their ritual practices so they could actually kill something. Roger and Maurice take pleasure in tormenting the littluns because they are smaller and weaker than they are. Even Piggy is impatient with their irrational fears, although he cares enough about them to act as their nurse-maid while the hunters go in search of the beast. Only Ralph and Simon show natural care for the youngest children, Simon out of saintliness and Ralph out of a sense of duty.

CHAPTER FIVE

Critical Analysis of the Novel

The great importance attributed by critics to William Golding's *Lord of the Flies* at first may seem out of proportion to its deceptively simplistic plot. Nonetheless, the book has inspired more critical response than perhaps any other novel before it and has been called by some the most important critical work of the 1950s, as well as of the twentieth century. Why did this short adventure novel about a group of boys stranded on an island gain so much attention? What is the significance of the book and why has it sustained the interest of critics for decades?

Many critics have argued that the critical significance of the novel resides in Golding's unusual combination of realistic elements and fable-like symbolism. Critics argued that Golding treated his subject honestly and realistically while at the same time instilling symbolic value into each element of the fiction, including setting, characters, dialog, and objects. In doing so, he created a text that works as a compelling psychological adventure story and allows for many levels of interpretation.

While the body of criticism on *Lord of the Flies* is vast and diverse, the most prevalent interpretations are based on reading the novel as an allegory, a story in which the various fictional

Jack threatens Ralph with his sharpened spear while Piggy looks on.

elements such as character, setting, objects, and plot symbolize some deeper, underlying meaning. Many critics have focused on the novel as a religious, political, or social allegory. While critics each approach the novel differently, overwhelmingly they reach the same fundamental, bleak conclusion—the same thesis that Golding purposely set out to demonstrate when writing the novel: that humanity is morally diseased and has the potential for great evil.

An Eden Allegory

Some critics who favor a religious interpretation of the novel say that *Lord of the Flies* is a biblical parable that deals with fundamental metaphysical questions that have always been of concern for religion: for instance, the nature of good and evil, the condition of humanity and its relationship to God, and the meaning of death and free will. These critics also frequently cite Golding's own religious beliefs to demonstrate how they influenced the novel.

In his adulthood, Golding became a Calvinist, a Protestant who believed in the tenets of the teachings of sixteenth-century Protestant reformer John Calvin. Broadly stated, the principles of Calvinism include a belief in predestination—the concept that human beings' fate and condition of salvation are determined by God and that there is nothing people can do to influence their fate.

Golding also believed in original sin, a Christian concept from the biblical story of Genesis which teaches that all people are born wicked because of the sin of Adam and Eve, who were cast out of the earthly paradise of the Garden of Eden for eating the forbidden fruit (an apple) from the tree of knowledge. According to the story, Adam and Eve's descendants, all of humanity, were born flawed because of this act, and humanity has been banished from paradise forever.

Critics argue that Golding brought his belief in original sin and predestination to *Lord of the Flies* by casting the story as an allegory of humans in the Garden of Eden. The boys, ignorant of their inherent potential for evil—their original sin—are fated to destroy the earthly paradise of the island.

Golding stranded his characters—all "innocent" children—on an idyllic island that many have likened to the Garden of Eden. The island's beauty, plentiful fruit, fresh water, material for shelter, and freedom from predators make it possible for the boys to live there indefinitely. As critic Francis Kearns writes, "It is, in short, a neatly Edenic situation where innocence may be tested."[84]

However, according to the biblical concept of original sin, innocence does not exist, as it was lost to humanity when Adam and Eve ate from the tree of knowledge and were cast out of Eden by God. According to Golding, innocence, in the context of *Lord of the Flies,* is actually ignorance of human nature. Golding wrote,

> [The boys on the island] don't understand their own nature and therefore, when they get to this island, they can look forward to a bright future, because they don't understand the things that threaten it. This seems to me to be innocence; I suppose you could almost equate it with ignorance of men's basic attributes.[85]

It is this ignorance of their nature as human beings that gets the boys into trouble. They do not understand their own potential for evil, and thus they allow their fears to destroy them. At first, the littluns speak of their fears and their nightmares, but the older boys dismiss them. However, as the novel progresses, some of the older boys, such as Maurice, begin to have doubts about whether there are beasts and ghosts. Once the pilot is discovered and mistaken for the beast, fear grips all of the boys—all except prophetic Simon, who understands that the beast is actually a manifestation of the boys' fears, their own morally diseased human nature made real.

This fear leads to death and the destruction of paradise. It is responsible for Simon's death and for Jack's ascendancy to power, which in turn is responsible for Piggy's murder and the attempted murder of Ralph. By the novel's conclusion, "Eden" is engulfed in flames, destroyed in an act of savagery as the boys use the fire to flush Ralph onto the beach to be killed. As critic Nicola Dicken-Fuller writes: "As a result [of their fears], death follows death and the Garden of Eden is lost to Man; the island can no longer be the paradise . . . that the boys had hoped for."[86]

Simon and the Beast

Critics favoring the novel as a religious allegory have also argued that Golding's portrayal of Simon is an intentional reference to important events in the biblical account of the life of Jesus. Simon functions as a prophet and saint in the novel. In his ability to discover the truth about the beast, he represents the boys' chance to redeem themselves from their fears and from savagery.

Like Jesus, Simon is kind, gentle, and helpful. He is one of the few boys who works with Ralph and Piggy on the shelters. He reaches fruit down from the high tree branches for the littluns, as Jesus fed his followers with loaves of bread and fishes in the Book of Matthew. Further, Simon is the only boy completely without fear. He frequently wanders into the jungle to be alone and think, just as, according to Luke 5:16, Jesus "withdrew himself into the wilderness, and prayed."

In addition, like Jesus, Simon is a prophet, one who is able to divine and reveal truth. He alone understands the nature of the evil on the island. (Some critics argue that Ralph comes to understand the nature of evil at the end of the novel, but, if so, this is only through experience rather than instinct or intuition, as with Simon.) Early on, when the others become fearful of "beasties" on the island, Simon suggests that "Maybe [the beast]'s only us."[87] He understands that the evil is from within humanity itself, that it is the boys' fears made real. However, the other boys cannot understand this comment because they are ignorant of their nature, and thus they do not listen to him.

Later, Simon goes into the forest near the mountain and encounters the Lord of the Flies in a scene that closely resembles the temptation of Jesus, as depicted in the biblical Book of Matthew. In Matthew, Jesus is led into the desert by God to be tempted by the devil. He fasts for forty days and forty nights and is met by the devil, who offers him kingdoms and wealth if Jesus will worship him. Matthew 4:8–10 says: "The devil took him to a very high mountain and showed him all the kingdoms of the world and their splendor. 'All this I will give you,' he said, 'if you will bow down and worship me.'" However, Jesus does not accept the devil's temptation. Instead, he sends the devil away and then sets off to begin his teachings. Similarly, in chapter 8 of *Lord of the Flies*, Simon goes into the jungle near the mountain where the boys have seen the beast. There, he suffers from the extreme heat and his intense thirst, but he maintains a vigil. From his hiding place, he observes Jack and the other hunters erect the pig's head on a stake as an offering to the beast.

After the hunters leave, Simon approaches the pig's head and falls into an epileptic seizure that causes him to hallucinate. In his vision, the pig's head reveals itself as the Lord of the Flies (which is the Hebrew translation of "Beelzebub," the prince of the devils in the Bible) and tells Simon that he is the reason that things are going wrong on the island. "You knew, didn't you?" said the Lord of the Flies. "I'm part of you? Close, close, close! I'm the reason why it's no go? Why things are what they are?"[88]

The beast tempts Simon with the idea of forgetting what he has discovered about evil—to be like the other boys. "'Come now,' said the Lord of the Flies. 'Get back to the others and we'll forget the whole thing.'"[89] Golding noted the significance of the temptation when he said, "This is, of course, the perennial temptation to the saint . . . to just go and be like ordinary men and let the whole thing slide. Instead of that, Simon goes up the hill."[90]

Defying temptation, Simon climbs the mountain to confront the beast. He is unafraid and understands the necessity of the act. "What else is there to do?"[91] he says. On the mountain, he discovers the dead pilot. Simon understands that the boys have created the beast out of their own fear: "The beast was harmless and horrible; and the news must reach the others as soon as possible."[92] He frees the pilot's parachute from the rocks so that the wind no longer thrashes the body around. Later, this also allows the pilot to blow free, eliminating the chance that the boys will discover for themselves what Simon has.

Simon rushes down the mountain to tell the others what he has discovered. He stumbles into Jack's feast where the boys are chanting and dancing with wild abandon around the fire in a ritual pig hunt. In a fury of hysteria and fear, the boys mistake Simon for the beast and brutally kill him. Afterward, his body washes away into the sea, destroying the evidence of the boys' crimes and allowing them—under Jack's guidance—to believe that the beast still lives.

According to this interpretation, Simon, like Jesus, dies for the sins of humanity. In the context of the novel, the sins are the fear and potential for destruction fundamental to the nature of human beings. Additionally, because Simon is unable to deliver his news—which would have been the boys' salvation—the fear of the beast and the destruction it brings with it only increases. Thus, as a parable of Jesus, *Lord of the Flies* is not optimistic. For as long as humanity is ignorant of its own morally diseased nature, there is no salvation.

Triumph of Fear

Other critics argue that *Lord of the Flies* is a political allegory. In this interpretation, three of the main characters in the novel—Ralph, Piggy, and Jack—represent abstract ideas about governing and power. The plot of the novel symbolically describes how, due to the essential flaws of humanity, oppressive forms of governing can arise out of even well-intentioned democratic societies.

Ralph symbolically represents law, order, and society. He is closely associated with the conch, a symbol of civilization and order and of great importance to the novel. Critic David Spitz writes that the boys elect Ralph as the leader not because he is the smartest boy (that is Piggy) or the one with the most experience (that is Jack) but primarily because of his association to the conch:

> Ralph is democratic man, the symbol of consent. . . .
> He was "set apart" not by virtue or intelligence or

other sign of personal superiority—though he may have well have been the tallest and strongest of the boys—but by the fact that it was he who had blown and possessed the conch, who had first exercised the symbol of legitimacy.[93]

Ralph's symbolic counterpart is Piggy. He represents rationality and common sense. Together, Ralph and Piggy attempt to create a civil society, one they imagine mimics the world of the grownups.

Like Ralph, Piggy is symbolically associated with the conch. Although Ralph discovers the shell, Piggy understands its significance. He cannot blow it himself, but he teaches Ralph to blow it for the first time, and this act establishes Ralph's position as leader.

Conversely, Jack represents despotic totalitarianism—a tyrannical form of government such as Hitler's fascist Nazi government or Stalin's brutal Communist government.

Some critics maintain that the novel's three main characters—Ralph, Piggy, and Jack— represent general truths about power and government.

Totalitarianism of this form demands total submission of the individual to the state and instills the leader with total power over the affairs and the people of the state. Like Hitler and Stalin, Jack desires power over others and wants them fearful and completely submissive to his authority.

In this interpretation of the novel, the opposition between Jack and Ralph represents the conflict between totalitarianism and democracy. Although Ralph and Jack initially like each other, the conflict between the boys' ideologies arises early. In chapter 3, while Jack hunts alone in the forest, Ralph attempts to organize the boys into a civil society. Frustrated by the lack of assistance he is getting from the boys, Ralph argues with Jack over the importance of hunting versus the importance of shelter and rescue.

"The best thing we can do is get ourselves rescued." [said Ralph].

Jack had to think for a moment before he could remember what rescue was.

"Rescue? Yes, of course! All the same, I'd like to catch a pig first—". . . Ralph looked at him critically through his tangle of fair hair.

"So long as your hunters remember the fire—"

"You and your fire!". . .

"Don't you want to be rescued? All you can talk about is pig, pig, pig!"

"But we want meat!". . .

They faced each other on the bright beach, astonished at the rub of feeling.[94]

This argument is the first of many between the two. The conflict between the boys becomes increasingly heated after

Jack (center) and his followers gather around the fire. According to some critics, Jack's character is a symbol of brutal totalitarian governments like those of Hitler and Stalin.

the first successful pig hunt. Jack takes the fire tenders with him on this hunt, allowing the fire to go out at the critical moment a ship passes the island and foiling their chance at rescue. Although he apologizes to Ralph, Jack is triumphant as a hunter and gets his first taste of power. At the feast, Jack revels in his power as chief hunter and leads the boys in the first ritual dance around the fire.

As Jack becomes increasingly successful as a hunter and as the fear of beasts becomes more prevalent, Jack's power grows. Like Hitler and Stalin, Jack uses fear to gain power and to rule. In governments the fear is usually of an enemy, either foreign or domestic; on the island, it is of the beast.

Jack tries to take Ralph's place as chief by democratic election, but when the littluns will not vote against Ralph, Jack leaves. He breaks away from Ralph's tribe to establish his own group, where he will be the unchallenged leader. He then wins over the boys with the promise of meat and protection from the beast.

The confrontations between Jack's and Ralph's groups grow increasingly hostile. Jack's tribe uses surprise attacks and fear to get what Jack wants from Ralph's group. They steal fire, then Piggy's specs. Finally, when Ralph takes Piggy and the twins, Sam and Eric, to Castle Rock, Roger tips the boulder and purposefully murders Piggy, simultaneously destroying the conch. In eliminating Piggy and the conch, this event removes two of the strongest symbols of civilization and order in the book. Jack orders the twins to be tied up and kidnapped, then he and the other hunters attack Ralph, intending to kill him. Ralph flees into the jungle, alone, a chief without a tribe.

At this point, Jack's rise to power is complete, and it has been achieved through fear and violence, just as the governments of despots like Hitler and Stalin. In his final act of destruction, Jack burns the island while Ralph hides. To the end a well-intentioned leader, Ralph recognizes that this act will destroy all the food on the island, leaving nothing for the children to eat the next day. Meanwhile, Jack is so short-sighted and obsessed with the idea of ridding the island of his former rival for power that he is willing to destroy everything and everyone to do so.

This political interpretation of the book highlights Golding's argument that man's fear can allow evil and destruction to arise even in the midst of well-intentioned democracies. As critic Howard S. Babb writes:

[Ralph's] good intentions, a capacity for leadership, and a commitment to social order will not suffice to prevent a reversion to savagery under pressure; and Jack [demonstrates] that fears, cruelty, and a lust for

power which inhabit every one of us can gain domi-
nance all too easily.[95]

Civilization Versus Nature

Some critics have seen Golding's portrayal of his characters'
reversion to savagery as a social allegory. According to these
critics, *Lord of the Flies* serves as an argument against the
centuries-old school of thought, sometimes referred to as
liberal humanism, which was based on a fundamental optimism about the goodness of humanity. To explain evil and
vice, some liberal humanists argued that humanity was naturally good but corrupted by the pressures and complexities
of civilization. This argument postulated a pristine, innocent, "natural" state in which humanity had lived before the
exertion of the forces of civilization, which include techno-
logical advancement and rationally ordered societies. Thus,
humanity could improve its condition through the elimina-
tion of these forces.

Taken to its extreme, this argument called for a return
of humanity to nature. By casting off the blandishments of
civilization, humanity would return to its innocent and
pristine state. To varying degrees, this idea influenced
many philosophers, writers, and other figures over the cen-
turies.

However, Golding's views on humanity opposed the liberal humanist point of view, and critics say that *Lord of the
Flies* is a social allegory that demonstrates the flaw in the liberal humanist argument. For Golding, far from being a cor-
rupting influence, civilization is the only thing that restrains
humanity from a life of barbarity. Golding places his characters on a pristine, idyllic island, where they are unsupervised
by adults and given complete freedom, which, in the context
of the novel, means freedom from the rules, norms, and
social responsibilities of civilization.

While the boys at first attempt to maintain their connection to civilization, freedom compels them away from it. Morally sick by nature and free to do as they choose without repercussions from the adult world, the boys grow increasingly barbaric and violent. Thus, as critic Patrick Reilly argues, "*Lord of the Flies* is essentially a critique of freedom."[96]

When the boys first arrive on the island, they are still strongly connected to civilization. They wear their school uniforms, resemble English schoolchildren, and try to emulate the manners and customs that have been taught to them by their culture. When Ralph blows the conch, they are drawn to it by convention, as they would be to a trumpet calling them to assembly in school. They come together and decide that, in the absence of adults, they will have to take care of themselves. They elect Ralph chief, in good part because he possesses the conch, the strongest symbol of civilization in the book. Under Ralph's leadership, the boys plan to fashion a society for themselves on the island. Duties are delegated—Jack and his choir become hunters to provide food—and rules are established, the first of which is the rule of the conch, which determines who may speak at the meetings.

Meanwhile, the boys' newfound freedom on the island is exciting and liberating. Without adults to supervise, guide, or punish, they are for the first time able to do whatever they please. However, the boys' freedom, unchecked by adult supervision, leads almost immediately to disaster. They set a fire on the mountain that grows out of control and kills one of the littluns. According to critics, this is only the first of three deaths on the island caused in one way or another by the boys' misguided freedom.

In the social allegory reading, Ralph and Piggy represent civilization. They are both associated with the conch, and they operate as a team trying to maintain order and society on the island. As leader, Ralph makes rules, organizes shelter, and tries to get the boys rescued with a signal fire. Piggy, the most adult of the boys, with his intelligence and his reverence for the adult world, is also the most adamant about maintaining civilization on the island. He assists Ralph in his leadership and persistently complains when rules are disobeyed.

Jack, Roger, and the rest of the hunters represent the will to freedom in the novel—the force that opposes civilization. However, even Jack at first shows that he is as indoctrinated as the others are in the social taboos and rules of civilized society. When he first encounters a pig, he is quite incapable of harming it, "because of the enormity of the knife descending and cutting into living flesh."[97] Even the delinquent Roger is at first restrained by the taboos of "parents and school and policemen and the law."[98]

However, the social restraints dissolve rapidly for Jack, Roger, and the other hunters. Although Jack is all for making rules, he is not interested in following them. He is the first to disobey the rule of the conch and becomes increasingly belligerent toward Ralph's leadership and antagonistic toward Piggy, who persists in complaining when he breaks the rules. Jack and the other boys want to hunt and have fun, and they take advantage of their freedom, particularly because it allows them to indulge their worst instincts. For example, in chapter 3, Roger and Maurice knock over the littluns' sandcastle, and Roger throws stones at one of the boys for fun. Each of the boys is aware of the retreat of civilization and the lack of repercussions for their actions, and it pleases them.

As the novel progresses, even the boys' physical appearances change as they descend into savagery. Their uniforms become dirty rags and their hair grows long and tangled. The hunters make the most dramatic transformation when they paint their faces, effectively masking their identities, which allows them to indulge increasingly in the pleasures of hunting, killing, and cruelty. By the end of the novel, the boys have become almost unrecognizable savages. Ralph is barely able to recognize Bill when he sees him on guard duty outside Castle Rock, and later, as the hunters chase Ralph through the jungle, he no longer distinguishes the boys by name.

Critics point out that Golding's novel does not uphold civilization as anything approaching perfection. Civilization itself taps the basic evil instincts of humanity to create sophisticated weapons of war. It is, after all, civilization and the world of adults that created the warplane responsible for their being on the island and for the nuclear weapons that have destroyed their homes. Nonetheless, according to this reading, the novel demonstrates that, without the restraints of civilization to control people, the inherent potential for evil within humanity will exercise itself through the errant freedom of even the young and innocent.

Not Without Hope

While critics have offered a variety of allegorical analyses of *Lord of the Flies*, the conclusions derived almost unanimously support Golding's pessimistic outlook on humanity. However, Golding and a few critics have pointed out that the novel is not without hope. While most criticism comes to the conclusion that Golding points to the faults of humanity without offering a solution, some critics see the existence of characters such as Ralph, Piggy, and Simon amid the Jacks and Rogers as evidence that Golding holds out some optimism about the human condition. Golding admitted that he was divided in his outlook. He wrote:

William Golding's view is that civilization is all that stands between ourselves and barbarism.

Jack stands by Ralph, who holds the conch. The large shell is symbolic of civilization and order.

I'm basically an optimist. Intellectually, I see man's balance is about fifty-fifty, and his chances of blowing himself up are about one to one. I can't see this any way but intellectually. I'm just emotionally unable to believe that he will do this. This means that I am by nature an optimist and by intellectual conviction a pessimist, I suppose.[99]

Notes

Introduction: The Lesson

1. William Golding, *The Hot Gates and Other Occasional Pieces.* New York: Pocket Books, 1967, p. 101.
2. Golding, *The Hot Gates and Other Occasional Pieces,* p. 85.
3. Golding, *The Hot Gates and Other Occasional Pieces,* p. 88.
4. Golding, *The Hot Gates and Other Occasional Pieces,* p. 85.
5. Khandkar Rezaur Rahman, *The Moral Vision of William Golding.* Dhaka, Bangladesh: University of Dhaka, 1990, p. 36.
6. Bernard S. Oldsey and Stanley Weintraub, *The Art of William Golding.* New York: Harcourt Brace and World, 1965, p. 19.
7. Herbert N. Foerstel, *Banned in the U.S.A.: A Reference Guide to Book Censorship in Schools and Public Libraries.* Westport, CT: Greenwood Press, 1994, p. 187.

Chapter 1: The Life of William Golding

8. Quoted in Mary Lynn Scott, "Universal Pessimist, Cosmic Optimist: William Golding," *Aurora Online,* 2001. http:// aurora.icaap.org.
9. Golding, *The Hot Gates and Other Occasional Pieces,* p. 175.
10. Golding, *The Hot Gates and Other Occasional Pieces,* p. 165.
11. Golding, *The Hot Gates and Other Occasional Pieces,* p. 167.
12. Quoted in William Golding, *Lord of the Flies: Casebook Edition,* ed. James R. Baker and Arthur P. Ziegler Jr. New York: Perigee Books, 1983, p. 226.
13. Golding, *The Hot Gates and Other Occasional Pieces,* p. 165.
14. Quoted in Oldsey and Weintraub, *The Art of William Golding,* p. 5.
15. Quoted in Golding, *Lord of the Flies: Casebook Edition,* p. 226.
16. Quoted John Carey, ed., *William Golding: The Man and His Books: A Tribute on His Seventy-Fifth Birthday.* London: Faber and Faber, 1986, p. 176.
17. Quoted in Oldsey and Weintraub, *The Art of William Golding,* p. 7.
18. Quoted in Carey, *William Golding,* p. 171.
19. Quoted in Lawrence S. Friedman, *William Golding.* New York: Continuum, 1993, p 12.

20. Golding, *The Hot Gates and Other Occasional Pieces*, p. 131.

21. Quoted in Friedman, *William Golding*, p. 12.

22. Judith Carver, interview by author, by e-mail, November 5–7, 2002.

23. Quoted in Carey, *William Golding*, p. 181.

24. Quoted in Oldsey and Weintraub, *The Art of William Golding*, p. 8.

25. Judith Carver, "Biography of William Golding," *William Golding*, 1997. www.william-golding.co.uk.

26. Quoted in Scott, "Universal Pessimist, Cosmic Optimist."

27. Quoted in Friedman, *William Golding*, p. 13.

28. Quoted in Oldsey and Weintraub, *The Art of William Golding*, p. 9.

29. Quoted in Carey, *William Golding*, p. 189.

30. Jonathan W. Doering, "The Fluctuations of William Golding's Critical Reputation," *Contemporary Review*, May 2002, p. 285.

31. Doering, "The Fluctuations of William Golding's Critical Reputation," p. 285.

32. Oldsey and Weintraub, *The Art of William Golding*, p. 11.

33. Quoted in Doering, "The Fluctuations of William Golding's Critical Reputation," p. 285.

34. James Wood, "Religious Insights of a Man Apart," *Manchester Guardian Weekly*, September 29, 1991, p. 25.

35. Quoted in Doering, "The Fluctuations of William Golding's Critical Reputation," p. 285.

Chapter 2: Historical Background of the Novel

36. Diane Andrews Henningfeld, "An Overview of *Lord of the Flies*," in *Exploring Novels*. Gale, InfoTrac College Edition, 1998. http://infotrac.thomsonlearning.com.

37. Pat Rogers, *An Outline of English Literature*. New York: Oxford University Press, 1992, p. 429.

38. Thomas R. Whissen, *Classic Cult Fiction: A Companion to Popular Cult Literature*. New York: Greenwood Press, 1992, p. 141.

39. Quoted in Nicola C. Dicken-Fuller, *William Golding's Use of Symbolism*. Sussex, UK: Bookbuild, 1990, p. 13.

40. Golding, *The Hot Gates and Other Occasional Pieces*, p. 86.

41. Golding, *The Hot Gates and Other Occasional Pieces*, p. 85.

42. Golding, *The Hot Gates and Other Occasional Pieces*, pp. 88–89.

43. Golding, *The Hot Gates and Other Occasional Pieces*, pp. 88–89.

44. Golding, *Lord of the Flies: Casebook Edition*, p. 201.

45. Quoted in Wood, "Religious Insights of a Man Apart," p. 25.

46. Whissen, *Classic Cult Fiction*, p. 143.

47. Bernard F. Dick, *William Golding*. Boston: Twayne, 1987, p. 146.

48. Dick, *William Golding*, p. 146.

49. Dick, *William Golding*, p. 146.

50. Quoted in Jack I. Biles and Robert O. Evans, *William Golding: Some Critical Considerations*. Lexington: University Press of Kentucky, 1978, p. 132.

51. Quoted in Dick, *William Golding*, p. 147.

Chapter 3: The Plot

52. William Golding, *Lord of the Flies*, New York: Perigee Books, 1954, p. 50.

53. Golding, *Lord of the Flies*, p. 51.

54. Golding, *Lord of the Flies*, p. 69.

55. Golding, *Lord of the Flies*, p. 82.

56. Golding, *Lord of the Flies*, p. 111.

57. Golding, *Lord of the Flies*, p. 118.

58. Golding, *Lord of the Flies*, p. 123.

59. Golding, *Lord of the Flies*, p. 127.

60. Golding, *Lord of the Flies*, p. 149.

61. Golding, *Lord of the Flies*, p. 152.

62. Golding, *Lord of the Flies*, p. 179.

63. Golding, *Lord of the Flies*, p. 180.

64. Golding, *Lord of the Flies*, p. 181.

Chapter 4: The Characters

65. Golding, *Lord of the Flies*, p. 183.

66. Golding, *Lord of the Flies*, p. 20.

67. Golding, *Lord of the Flies*, p. 31.

68. Golding, *Lord of the Flies*, p. 51.

69. Golding, *Lord of the Flies*, p. 63.

70. Golding, *Lord of the Flies*, p. 21.

71. Golding, *Lord of the Flies*, p. 33.

72. Golding, *Lord of the Flies*, p. 65.

73. Golding, *Lord of the Flies*, p. 180.

74. Golding, *Lord of the Flies*, p. 10.

75. Golding, *Lord of the Flies*, p. 115.

76. Golding, *Lord of the Flies*, p. 202.

77. Golding, *Lord of the Flies*, p. 22.

78. Golding, *Lord of the Flies*, p. 60.

79. Golding, *Lord of the Flies*, p. 180.

80. Golding, *Lord of the Flies*, p. 190.

81. Golding, *Lord of the Flies*, p. 19.

82. Golding, *Lord of the Flies*, p. 96.

83. Golding, *Lord of the Flies*, p. 24.

Chapter 5: Critical Analysis of the Novel

84. Quoted in William Nelson, ed., *William Golding's* Lord of the Flies: *A Source Book*. New York: Odyssey Press, 1963, p. 151.

85. Golding, *Lord of the Flies: Casebook Edition*, p. 190.

86. Dicken-Fuller, *William Golding's Use of Symbolism*, p. 16.

87. Golding, *Lord of the Flies*, p. 89.

88. Golding, *Lord of the Flies*, p. 142.

89. Golding, *Lord of the Flies*, p. 143.

90. Quoted in Golding, *Lord of the Flies: Casebook Edition*, p. 192.

91. Golding, *Lord of the Flies*, p. 145.

92. Golding, *Lord of the Flies*, p. 142.

93. David Spitz, "Power and Authority: An Interpretation of Golding's *Lord of the Flies*," *Antioch Review*, Spring 1970, p. 21.

94. Golding, *Lord of the Flies*, p. 54.

95. Howard S. Babb, *Novels of William Golding*. Columbus: Ohio State University Press, 1970, pp. 30–31.

96. Patrick Reilly, Lord of the Flies: *Fathers and Sons*. New York: Twayne, 1992, p. 69.

97. Golding, *Lord of the Flies*, p. 31.

98. Golding, *Lord of the Flies*, p. 62.

99. Golding, *Lord of the Flies: Casebook Edition*, p. 191.

For Further Exploration

Below are some suggestions for potential essays on *Lord of the Flies*.

1. William Golding called his novel a fable, a form traditionally featuring animals, such as Aesop's "The Tortoise and the Hare" or George Orwell's *Animal Farm*. If you were to rewrite Golding's novel with animals in the place of human characters, which animal would each character become and why? What characteristics do each of Golding's characters possess that would make them like a particular animal? How would substituting animals in the place of humans affect the novel's themes and meanings? *See also* William Golding, "A Fable." In *The Hot Gates and Other Occasional Pieces*. London: Faber and Faber, 1965; Mark Kinkead-Weekes and Ian Gregor, *William Golding, A Critical Study*. London: Faber and Faber, 1970.

2. The symbolism of objects, characters, and setting plays an important role in *Lord of the Flies*. Selecting one of the main characters, discuss how the symbols associated with the character affects your understanding of his role in the novel. *See also* Samuel Hynes, *William Golding*. 2nd ed. New York: Columbia University Press, 1968; Nicola C. Dicken-Fuller, *William Golding's Use of Symbolism*. Sussex, UK: Bookbuild, 1990.

3. One of the reasons Golding chose schoolboys as characters in *Lord of the Flies* was that he was frustrated with what he saw as the inaccurate portrayal of children in Victorian literature. He felt he understood how real children behaved from his experiences as a schoolmaster and a person. He wrote, in *The Hot Gates and Other Occasional Pieces*, "I was well situated for this, since at the time I was teaching them. Moreover, I am a son, brother, and father. I have lived for many years with small boys, and understand and know them with an awful precision." Do you think Golding's portrayal of the boys in *Lord of the Flies* is realistic? If Golding were to write his novel today, what changes would you suggest he make in the portrayal? *See also* Patrick Reilly, Lord of the Flies: *Fathers and Sons*. New York: Twayne, 1992.

4. While Golding describes Ralph as "no devil," it is clear from several scenes in the novel that he shares some of the same impulses and feelings as Jack and the hunters have. What keeps Ralph from becoming like Jack and the other hunters? Is the influence of Piggy significant in this regard? What would have happened in the novel if Ralph had given in to violent impulses and actions and become like Jack, Roger, and the others? *See also* Patrick

Reilly, "*Lord of the Flies:* Beelzebub's Boys." In *The Literature of Guilt: From "Gulliver" to Golding.* Iowa City: University of Iowa Press, 1988.

5. In the novel Ralph's frustration becomes evident when the boys will not organize and help do the simplest or most necessary chores. In contrast, Jack has them organized for hunting, providing him water, working guard duty, and even willing to kill at his command. How is Jack's leadership different from Ralph's? What characteristics do they have in common? What characteristics are different and why is Jack able to organize the boys while Ralph cannot? *See also* David Spitz, "Power and Authority: An Interpretation of Golding's *Lord of the Flies,*" *Antioch Review,* Spring 1970; John M. Egan, "Golding's View of Man." In William Nelson, ed., *William Golding's* Lord of the Flies: *A Source Book.* New York: Odyssey Press, 1963; Patrick Reilly, "*Lord of the Flies:* Beelzebub's Boys." In *The Literature of Guilt: From "Gulliver" to Golding.* Iowa City: University of Iowa Press, 1988.

6. Simon and Piggy are each described in the novel as different from the other boys. Discuss how the two characters function in the novel as outsiders. What, if anything, is the significance of the fact that they are both killed by the other boys? *See also* Patrick Reilly, Lord of the Flies: *Fathers and Sons.* New York: Twayne, 1992.

7. In recent years, some groups have attempted to have *Lord of the Flies* banned from school and public libraries, charging that its pessimistic themes are unsuitable for young readers. Others have defended the book by saying that it presents readers with the opportunity to think about questions about the nature of good and evil, society and savagery, and other important issues. Which of these points of view do you agree with? Discuss why, supporting your argument with examples from the novel. *See also* Herbert N. Foerstel, *Banned in the U.S.A.: A Reference Guide to Book Censorship in Schools and Public Libraries.* Westport, CT: Greenwood Press, 2002.

8. Some critics have complained that the ending of *Lord of the Flies* is too neat because of the surprise rescue. However, others have argued that, for Ralph, the rescue is actually no rescue at all because the naval officer is an adult hunter, akin to Jack. Discuss the ending of the novel and what the ending means. *See also* Arnold Johnston, *Of Earth and Darkness: The Novels of William Golding.* Columbia: University of Missouri Press, 1980; Patrick Reilly, "*Lord of the Flies:* Beelzebub's Boys." In *The Literature of Guilt: From "Gulliver" to Golding.* Iowa City: University of Iowa Press, 1988.

Appendix of Criticism

An Unpleasant Story, Skillfully Told

Mr. William Golding has found for his first novel a situation with which no one who writes as well as he does could go wrong. He has imagined a parcel of boys of roughly prep-school age . . . set down and abandoned on an uninhabited Pacific island. . . . Mr. Golding's boys are under the stress of night-terrors and the leadership of a boy who in other circumstances might have been a modern [hero], they lapse into barbarism. Piggy, the clever boy of the outfit, lower-class, fat, asthmatic, short-sighted to the point of blindness, is killed, and Ralph, the responsible one, the born prefect, is hunted like an animal. *Lord of the Flies* is like a fragment of a nightmare, for all that it is lightly told. It commands a reluctant assent: yes, doubtless it could be like that, with the regression from choir school to Mau Mau only a step. The difficulty begins when one smells allegory. "There's not a child so small and weak But has his little cross to take." These children's crosses, it seems to me, were altogether too unnaturally heavy for it to be possible to draw conclusions from Mr. Golding's novel, and if that is so, it is, however, skillfully told, only a rather unpleasant and too-easily affecting story.

Walter Allen, "New Novels." In William Nelson, ed.,
William Golding's Lord of the Flies: *A Source Book.*
New York: Odyssey Press, 1963.

Lord of the Flies Under Rigorous Scrutiny

It is clear from the start of William Golding's *Lord of the Flies* . . . that it would be insulting to judge it by any but the most rigorous standards. . . . The weaknesses of the novel may be summed up as a tendency to be too explicit. At times the boys are less boys than archetypal savages producing the correct taboos a little too promptly, at times the metaphors—as in "authority sat on his shoulder and chattered in his ear like an ape"—underline the sense a little too neatly. Perhaps, too, the slaughtered pig's head adopts Beelzebub's name of Lord of the Flies too easily in the mind of the delirious little boy and tells him too dogmatically that the Beast which they all fear is part of themselves. But these reservations come only on reflection when the book is subjected to the most exacting scrutiny; its progress from the beginning when the little boy stands on his head in joy at being on a real desert island to the end when, rescued physically, he weeps "for the end of innocence, the darkness of man's heart" is magnificent.

Douglas Hewitt, "New Novels." In William Nelson, ed.,
William Golding's Lord of the Flies: *A Source Book.*
New York: Odyssey Press, 1963.

Fable

Fables are those narratives which leave the impression that their purpose was anterior, some initial thesis or contention which they are apparently concerned to embody and express in concrete terms. Fables always give the impression that they were preceded by the conclusion which it is their function to draw. . . .

[At the end of *Lord of the Flies* the] abrupt return to childhood, to insignificance, underscores the argument of the narrative: that Evil is inherent in the human mind itself, whatever innocence may cloak it, ready to put forth its strength as soon as the occasion is propitious. This is Golding's theme, and it takes on a frightful force by being presented in juvenile terms, in a setting that is twice deliberately likened to the sunny Coral Island of R.M. Ballantyne. The boys' society represents, in embryo, the society of the adult world, their impulses and convictions are those of adults incisively abridged, and the whole narrative is a powerfully ironic commentary on the nature of Man, an accusation leveled at us all. . . . Like any orthodox moralist Golding insists that Man is a fallen creature, but he refuses to hypostatize Evil or to locate it in a dimension of its own. On the contrary, Beelzebub, Lord of the Flies, is Roger and Jack and you and I, ready to declare himself as soon as we permit him to.

The intentness with which this thesis is developed leaves no doubt that the novel is a fable, a deliberate translation of a proposition into the dramatized terms of art, and as usual we have to ask ourselves how resourceful and complete the translation has been, how fully the thesis has been absorbed and rendered implicit in the tale as it is told. . . .

John Peter, "The Fables of William Golding,"
Kenyon Review, Autumn, 1957, pp. 577–92.

The Novel's Setting

Fable-like, time and place [in *Lord of the Flies*] are vague. The Queen (Elizabeth?) still reigns, and "Reds" are apparently the vague enemy. It is the postcatastrophic near-future, in which nuclear war has laid waste to much of the West. ("They're all dead," Piggy thinks. And "civilization," corroborates Golding, is "in ruins.") The fiery crash of the boys' plane upon a tropical island has been the final stage of their evacuation from England. The island seems to lie somewhere in the Indian or Pacific Ocean, probably on a line extending from England to Australia, which could well have been the planned terminus of their evacuation. Jack provides the clue for such geographical extrapolation when he speaks of Simon's seizures at "Gib." (Gibraltar) and "Addis" (Addis Ababa), as well as "at matins over the precentor." . . .

If there were an end-paper map for Golding's island, it would no doubt be marked to indicate these major points of interest: (1) the beach along the lagoon, where Piggy and Ralph find the conch, and where assemblies are held near a natural platform of fallen trees; (2) the mountaintop, from which the island is surveyed, where the signal fire is placed, and where eventually the dead parachutist is trapped by wind and rock; (3) the burned out quarter mile, where the mulberry-faced boy dies in the first fire; (4) Simon's leafy bower, to which he makes mystic retreats and from which he views the ceremony of impaling the pig's head upon a stake; (5) the orchard, where the fruit is picked and where some of the "littluns" are "taken short," leaving behind their fecal trail; (6) the "castle" at the tail end of the island, rising a hundred feet from the sea, where the first search for the "beast" is made, and where Piggy is killed after Jack has made this bastion his headquarters; and (7) the jungle, with its hanging vines that recall snakes and "beasties," with its pig trails where Jack hunts and where Ralph is finally hunted.

When the details are extracted and given order under an analytical light, Golding's island looks naturalistic in specification. But matters are not all that clear in the book. The location of the island, for example, is kept deliberately vague: it is sufficiently removed to draw only two ships in a month or so, yet close enough to "civilization" to be the floor above which deadly, and old-fashioned, air battles are fought. . . . And Golding's graphically novelistic character and topographic details, both poetic and naturalistic, tend to blur the famous qualities of the narrative's use of time and setting in its opening and close. Although it is enough to say that the fabulist must be permitted pegs upon which to hang his fable, it is Golding's richly novelistic elements of the telling that call attention to the subtle dissonance. Paradoxically—yet artistically—this very tension between realistic novel and allegorical fable imparts to *Lord of the Flies* some of its unique power.

Bernard S. Oldsey and Stanley Weintraub, "Beelzebub Revisited:
Lord of the Flies." In *The Art of William Golding.*
New York: Harcourt Brace and World, 1965.

The Enemy Within

To realize his purpose Golding patterned his book after a nineteenth century work on a related theme, R.M. Ballantyne's *The Coral Island*, whose three characters carried the same names as some of the protagonists in *Lord of the Flies*. In this way, he thought, he could show that little had changed though much had changed in that century. He chose British schoolboys because, as he said, he knew them best; he had himself been a schoolmaster for many years and because they were the stuff of which British gentlemen were made; hence it was to be expected that they would know how to conduct themselves.

He removed them from civil society and isolated them on a remote island, an earthly paradise, beautiful and with an abundance of food, water, and the materials for shelter. He kept them below the age of overt sex, for he wished to exclude this issue as a causal factor. He excluded too private property and the struggle for survival, neither work nor robbery was essential for existence, and hence avoided the controversy that engaged [critics] over the Robinson Crusoe story: whether political power (force) or economic power (exploitation) should be given the higher priority. Along with Freud and Marx and Darwin, he banished Caesar; for there was no danger of external aggression and hence no need for an army. Finally, there were no classes, no divisions, no inequalities based on previous status; except for Jack, who initially appears as the head of a group of uniformed choirboys, a relationship and a dress that are quickly terminated, the only significant sign of difference is that of age.

Everything, then, was there for a calm and peaceful and contented life. It was a veritable utopia: Here at last was the imagined but never fully realized place leaping into real life. It was, if you will, a state of nature inhabited by free and equal individuals. If anything were to go wrong, as it tragically did, it could only come, then, from within; the only enemy of man was himself.

David Spitz, "Power and Authority:
An Interpretation of Golding's *Lord of the Flies*,"
Antioch Review, Spring, 1970, pp. 21–33.

Point of View and Structure of the Novel

The story of *Lord of the Flies* is told from the omniscient point of view. Golding as narrator shifts from one boy to another, among the major characters, telling each one's thoughts and decisions, explaining his motivations and reactions, or seeing a situation with his perspective; and at the very end he shifts away from the boys to their adult rescuer. Occasionally, at certain crucial times when the context of the novel calls for an objective, uninvolved voice to be heard as the voice of truth, Golding stands back from the action and comments unobtrusively on the situation. For the most part, however, the story develops through dramatic action and dialogue, not through authorial exposition and comment; and this method contrasts with the moralizing first-person narration of *The Coral Island*, which Golding is "correcting." He perhaps felt that readers familiar with the Ballantyne story would be aware of this contrast. Instead of telling, then, Golding is showing; and the difference in this technique is as significant as the contrast between the two writers' attitudes toward their material.

The omniscient point of view is another device for widening the scope of the novel, for obviously a part of the whole plan of the narrative is that the attitudes of each of the four principal characters—Ralph, Jack, Piggy, Simon—be included. This particular point of view—the omniscient—is, furthermore, appropriate and important to the novel in that it can control and unify both what happens on the island and what is happening in the world surrounding it. This fictional device is capable of producing an over-all irony that another device could hardly so economically and directly create. The identification of the dead parachutist, for instance, and the information about where he comes from and why, would be impossible without the omniscient point of view; and the kind of irony that derives from the contrast between the reader's knowledge of the true situation and the characters' ignorance of it would have been otherwise unobtainable.

E.C. Bufkin, "*Lord of the Flies:* An Analysis,"
Exploring Novels. Gale, InfoTrac College Edition, 1998.
http://infotrac.thomsonlearning.com.

A "Vulgar" Book?

Lord of the Flies has earned for itself and its author great critical acclaim. It has also been extolled by teachers for the excitement it can engender in readers and as a work in which the motivation of characters is readily understood by adolescent readers. Despite these accolades for the novel as a work of literary art and as a teaching tool, *Lord of the Flies* has on occasion aroused the ire of would-be censors.

Some have opposed the use of the novel in the classroom because of the use of "vulgar" language. Certain words, notably "sucks," "ass," and the British slang word "bloody," are used. It is patently obvious that there is no prurient motivation behind the author's choice of these words. Not one of these words is ever used outside of a context in which the word appears to be quite naturally the word the character would use. The choir boys may well sing like "angels," as is stated; nevertheless, these are perfectly normal pre-adolescent boys. Given the proclivities of such youth the world over, verisimilitude would be lost had they, amongst themselves, always spoken like angels.

The sexual symbolism of the killing of the sow has also raised some puritanical brows. This violent scene is described in terms which might well be used to describe a rape. Such symbolism is fully justified, however, if the author is to be allowed to make his point that the motivation of the boys, casting away the cloak of civilization, is no longer merely securing food. Rather, they have moved from serving practical needs to an insane lust for working their will upon other creatures. The next step is the slaughter of their own kind.

Objection, too, has come upon that very point: children killing children. One must remind those who object to this violence that this piece of literature is a parable. Children are specifically used to show that even the innocence of childhood can be corrupted by fears from within. Those who would deny Golding this mode of establishing his theme would deny to all authors the right to make their point in an explicit fashion.

The most vociferous denunciation of *Lord of the Flies* has been vocalized by those who have misread the book to the point that they believe it deals with Satanism. The symbolism of the title, which is the English translation of the Greek word "Beelzebub," is surely being misinterpreted by such folk. In fact, theologian Davis Anderson states unequivocally that "Golding is a Christian writer." Anderson defines the central theme of *Lord of the Flies* as a statement of what it is like to experience the fall from innocence into sin and to experience damnation. Thus, a theologian sees the novel as one dealing with the Christian doctrine of original sin and of the rupture of man's relationship with God! Consequently, one who would attack this novel as an exercise in Satanism assuredly holds an indefensible premise.

> Paul Slayton, "Teaching Rationale for William Golding's
> *Lord of the Flies.*" In Nicholas J. Karolides, Lee Burress,
> John M. Kean, eds., *Censored Books: Critical Viewpoints.*
> Scarecrow Press, 1993, pp. 351–57.

Civilization and Chaos

The theme of the book is that the human condition is irrational. Man has no nature, but rather is an excrescence from chaotic, cruel and blind forces which are violent and yet meaningless. Man springs forth from these forces and regresses into them. The violence which develops on the island only reflects in microcosm the violence of the rest of the world: the boys appear on the island as the result of some atomic catastrophe, the sole intruder on the island is the dead pilot who is shot down from the firmament overhead, and the boys leave the island in the company of armed men traveling in a warship. When all is said and done, man's condition is represented as something hateful. Thus the novel is representative of the spirit of much of modern thought and art.

Ralph's obsession with maintaining fire is symbolic of man's illusion that civilization will bring salvation. The usage of fire to symbolize the arts and sciences of civilization was canonized in the Prometheus legend, and a reflection of that myth is found in the book when the forces of chaos plan to steal back the fire. Civilization, however, is merely a momentary veneer which ill conceals man's essential nature. Under pressure, even Ralph, the protagonist of civilization, begins to revert to his primal condition, forgetting the importance of the fire.

Almost immediately after the boys' arrival on the island, the forces of violence, blind power and cruelty, typified by Jack, Roger, and their associates, begin to struggle to attain ascendancy over the values of civilization and traditional authority, represented by the fire and Ralph with his conch. These boys hanker for violence and a return to the primordial chaos, typified by the hunt. Soon their antagonism becomes hostility, as the hunt and blood-lust become responsible for the fire dying out and the chance for a return to civilization being missed. It is at this time, significantly, that the specter of some mysterious beast begins to loom up before the boys. The beast becomes a source of terror and division among them as fear grows of some unchained and superior force in their midst.

John M. Egan, "Golding's View of Man."
In William Nelson, ed., *William Golding's*
Lord of the Flies: *A Source Book.*New York:
Odyssey Press, 1963.

Evil in Children

Lord of the Flies is a fascinating tale like the island story of *Robinson Crusoe,* with the difference that the characters of Golding's novel are all children. The novel may resemble certain children's books like *The Wind in the Willows, High Wind in Jamaica, Green Mansions,* and other works of juvenile literature. These children's classics usually present a romantic view of the children, their adventure and survival; they also depict the idyllic existence of the Rousseauistic noble savage without the taint of sin; they portray the beauty of nature symbolizing a deep yearning of the soul for the attainment of love and beauty in life. Golding turns this tradition upside down by introducing evil in the nature of children.

> Khandkar Rezaur Rahman,
> *The Moral Vision of William Golding.*
> Dhaka, Bangladesh: University of Dhaka, 1990.

Genre Conventions of *Lord of the Flies*

Golding has founded *Lord of the Flies* on a number of more or less current conventions. First of all, he has used the science fiction convention of setting his action in the future, thus substituting the eventually probable for the immediately actual, and protecting his fable from literalistic judgments of details or of credibility. . . . The boys land unharmed on a desert island. At this point, a second literary convention enters. The desert island tale shares certain literary quality with science fiction. Both offer a "what-would-happen-if" situation, in which real experience is simplified in order that certain values and problems may be regarded in isolation. Both tend to simplify human moral issues by externalizing good and evil; both offer occasions for Utopian fantasies.

> Samuel Hynes, *William Golding.*
> 2nd ed. New York: Columbia University Press, 1968.

Chronology

1911
William Gerald Golding born in Newquay, Cornwall, England, on September 19.

1930
Golding enrolls at Brasenose College at Oxford to study science.

1933
Golding changes major to English literature at Oxford.

1934
Golding publishes a book of poems, called *Poems*.

1935
Golding works with theater groups in London, takes teaching post at Michael Hall in Streatham, South London.

1937
Golding quits post at Michael Hall, returns to Oxford to acquire teaching qualification.

1938
Golding moves to Maidstone, Kent, to teach at Maidstone Grammar School.

1939
Golding marries Mabel Ann Brookfield.

1940
Golding begins teaching at Bishop Wordsworth School in Salisbury, Wiltshire. Teaching interrupted by beginning of World War II. Golding enlists as seaman in Royal Navy.

1940–1945
Golding serves in various posts during World War II, attaining rank of lieutenant, commanding his own ship, and participating in significant battles such as the D day invasion of Normandy in 1944.

1945
In autumn Golding returns to teach at Bishop Wordsworth School and begins writing novels. United States drops atomic bombs on Japanese cities of Nagasaki and Hiroshima.

1949
Soviet Union conducts first successful atom bomb tests, heating up Cold War between U.S.S.R. and United States.

1954

Lord of the Flies published in the United Kingdom by Faber and Faber.

1955

First American edition of *Lord of the Flies* published by Coward-McCann; Golding's second novel, *The Inheritors*, is published.

1956

Golding's third novel, *Pincher Martin*, is published; his novella *Envoy Extraordinary* is published in *Sometimes, Never: Three Tales of Imagination*.

1959

Golding's fourth novel, *Free Fall*, is published.

1961

Golding retires from teaching at Bishop Wordsworth School after fifteen years' service to write full time.

1962

First American mass-market paperback edition of *Lord of the Flies* published by Coward-McCann; *Lord of the Flies* becomes a best-seller in the United States; Golding takes a one-year writer-in-residence position at Hollins College in Virginia.

1963

First film version of *Lord of the Flies* released, directed by Peter Brook.

1964

Golding's fifth novel, *The Spire*, is published.

1965

Golding's first collection of essays, *The Hot Gates and Other Occasional Pieces*, is published.

1967

Golding's sixth novel, *The Pyramid*, is published.

1970

Talk: Conversations with William Golding, a collection of interviews between Golding and critic Jack I. Biles, is published with a foreword written by Golding.

1971

Golding's collection of novellas, *The Scorpion God*, is published.

1979
Golding's seventh novel, *Darkness Visible*, is published.

1980
Golding's eighth novel, *Rates of Passage*, is published.

1982
Golding's second collection of essays, *A Moving Target*, is published.

1983
First casebook edition of *Lord of the Flies* released by Putnam in the United States; Golding wins Nobel Prize for literature.

1984
Golding's ninth novel, *The Paper Men*, is published.

1985
Golding and wife Ann move from Wiltshire to Cornwall; Golding's third collection of essays, *An Egyptian Journal*, is published.

1987
Golding's tenth novel, *Close Quarters*, is published.

1988
Golding knighted by Queen Elizabeth II.

1989
Golding's eleventh novel, *Fire Down Below*, is published.

1990
Second film version of *Lord of the Flies* released. American version, directed by Harry Hook, substitutes American military cadets for English schoolboys.

1993
William Golding dies at home in Truro, Cornwall.

1995
Golding's twelfth novel, *Double Tongue*, is published posthumously from a working draft extant at the time of his death.

Works Consulted

Major Editions of *Lord of the Flies*

William Golding, *Lord of the Flies*. London: Faber and Faber, 1954.

———, *Lord of the Flies*. New York: Coward-McCann, 1955.

———, *Lord of the Flies: A Novel*. Introduction by E.M. Forster, with a biographical and critical note by E.L. Epstein. New York: Riverhead Books, 1997.

———, *Lord of the Flies: Casebook Edition*, James R. Baker and Arthur P. Ziegler Jr. New York: Perigee Books, 1983.

Also by William Golding

William Golding, *The Inheritors*. London: Faber and Faber, 1955. The story of a group of Neanderthals who encounter a new race, Homo sapiens, whose skills and sophistication as well their cruelty, sense of guilt, and incipient corruption spell doom for the simpler, more gentle Neanderthals.

———, *Pincher Martin*. London: Faber and Faber, 1956. (Also known as *The Two Deaths of Christopher Martin*. New York: Harcourt Brace, 1957.) The sole survivor of a torpedoed destroyer is cast upon a huge, barren rock in the mid-Atlantic and struggles to survive and maintain his sanity.

———, *Freefall*. London: Faber and Faber, 1959. Artist Sammy Mountjoy looks back over his past to find the event that changed his life.

———, *The Spire*. London: Faber and Faber, 1964. The story about the construction of a cathedral spire. Jocelyn, dean of a cathedral, has decided to erect a four-hundred-foot spire before his death. However, its construction creates sacrifice, treachery, and murder.

———, *The Hot Gates and Other Occasional Pieces*. New York: Pocket Books, 1967. This collection of nonfiction includes Golding's first published autobiographical essays as well as essays on various literary and historical figures and events.

———, *The Pyramid*. London: Faber and Faber, 1967. A light, comic portrayal of Oliver, an eighteen-year-old boy bound for the university who wants to enjoy himself before going off to school—a difficult task in his small English town where everyone knows everyone else's business.

———, *The Scorpion God: Three Short Novels*. London: Faber and Faber, 1971. Three novellas thematically linked by their exploration of the emergence of new forms of consciousness and, hence, new forms of society. The novellas include "Clonk Clonk," set in prehistoric Africa, Golding's previously published "Envoy Extraordinary," and the titular novella "The Scorpion God," set in ancient Egypt at the time of the first pharaohs.

———, *Darkness Visible*. New York: Farrar, Straus, Giroux, 1979. A novel exploring the intertwining destinies of three children after the London blitz during World War II.

———, *Rites of Passage*. New York: Farrar, Straus, Giroux, 1980. The first volume in a trilogy, including *Close Quarters* and *Fire Down Below*, portraying life aboard an ancient ship at the end of the Napoleonic Wars. This novel won Golding the prestigious Booker Prize.

———, *A Moving Target*. London: Faber and Faber, 1982. A collection of short nonfiction essays, originally delivered by Golding as lectures or written for magazines and newspapers, reflecting on places he had lived and traveled in, as well as ideas about history, culture, and literature, including his own writing.

———, *The Paper Men*. New York: Farrar, Straus, Giroux, 1984. A dark, satiric novel depicting the battle between a world-famous English novelist and an American academic who has decided to write his biography, even if he has to kill the novelist to do so.

———, *An Egyptian Journal*. Boston: Faber and Faber, 1985. Golding's account of his travels in Egypt.

———, *Close Quarters*. New York: Farrar, Straus, Giroux, 1987. The second volume in a trilogy, including *Rites of Passage* and *Fire Down Below*, portraying life aboard an ancient ship at the end of the Napoleonic Wars.

———, *Fire Down Below*. New York: Farrar, Straus, Giroux, 1989. The third volume in a trilogy, including *Rites of Passage* and *Close Quarters*, portraying life aboard an ancient ship at the end of the Napoleonic Wars.

———, *The Double Tongue*. London: Faber and Faber, 1995. Set in ancient Greece, this novel, left in draft form at Golding's death and published posthumously, depicts a Delphic oracle who witnesses the rise of Roman power and the retreat of the Hellenistic culture.

Film Adaptations of *Lord of the Flies*

Lord of the Flies. United Kingdom: Lewis Allen, 1963.
Lord of the Flies. United States: Castle Rock Entertainment, 1990.

Biographies and Interviews

Jack Biles and William Golding, *Talk: Conversations with William Golding*. Foreword by William Golding. New York: Harcourt Brace Jovanovich, 1970. Interviews about Golding's life and work.

John Carey, ed., *William Golding: The Man and His Books: A Tribute on His Seventy-Fifth Birthday*. London: Faber and Faber, 1986. A collection of essays on Golding and his major works.

Judith Carver, "Biography of William Golding," *William Golding*, 1997. www.william-golding.co.uk. A website with biographical content provided by Golding's daughter Judith Carver.

Judith Carver. Interview by author. By e-mail, November 5–7, 2002. Correspondence provided ample and insightful information about Golding's life.

Mary Lynn Scott, "Universal Pessimist, Cosmic Optimist: William Golding," *Aurora Online*, 2001. http://aurora.icaap.org. An interview of William Golding given in 1984 after the publication of *The Paper Men*.

Literary Criticism

Howard S. Babb, *Novels of William Golding*. Columbus: Ohio State University Press, 1970. An analysis of *Lord of the Flies* exploring the psychological, political, social, and religious allegorical elements in the text.

James R. Baker, ed., *Critical Essays on William Golding*. Boston: G.K. Hall, 1988. A diverse compilation of essays on William Golding's novels.

Jack I. Biles and Robert O. Evans, *William Golding: Some Critical Considerations*. Lexington: University Press of Kentucky, 1978. This collection of essays includes some of the most frequently referenced critical work on Golding.

S.J. Boyd, *The Novels of William Golding*. 2d ed. New York: Harvester Wheatsheaf, 1988. An enthusiastic guide to the major novels of William Golding.

E.C. Bufkin, "*Lord of the Flies:* An Analysis," *Exploring Novels*. Gale, InfoTrac College Edition, 1998. http://infotrac.thomsonlearning.com. In this article Bufkin asserts that, in *Lord of the Flies*, Golding reworks the Christian myth of the Fall of Man, principally through the literary device of irony.

Bernard F. Dick, *William Golding*. Boston: Twayne, 1987. A biographical and literary analysis of Golding and his work.

Nicola C. Dicken-Fuller, *William Golding's Use of Symbolism*. Sussex, UK: Bookbuild, 1990. This volume contains essays, each discussing the symbols and icons in each of Golding's novels.

Lawrence S. Friedman, *William Golding*. New York: Continuum, 1993. Critical essays on Golding's novels, from *Lord of the Flies* to *The Paper Men*, including a literary-biographical history of Golding's writing.

Diane Andrews Henningfeld, "An Overview of *Lord of the Flies*," *Exploring Novels*. Gale, InfoTrac College Edition, 1998. http://infotrac.thomsonlearning.com. This brief article provides biographical information on William Golding and concise literary analysis of *Lord of the Flies*.

Samuel Hynes, *William Golding*. 2nd ed. New York: Columbia University Press, 1968. A critical study of Golding's first five novels.

Arnold Johnston, *Of Earth and Darkness: The Novels of William Golding*. Columbia: University of Missouri Press, 1980. Literary analysis of William Golding's major works, including influences, character analysis, and themes.

Mark Kinkead-Weekes and Ian Gregor, *William Golding: A Critical Study*. London: Faber and Faber, 1970. Critical essays on Golding's first five novels, as well as a chapter summarizing his later work through the mid-1980s.

Arnold Kruger, "Golding's *Lord of the Flies*," *Explicator*, Spring 1999. A study of the character of Simon in *Lord of the Flies* as an analogue of the biblical Simon, an apostle of Jesus.

Stephen Medcalf, *William Golding*. Essex, UK: Longman Group, 1975. Part of the British Council's Writers and Their Work series, this short volume contains biographical information as well as an analysis of Golding's writings until the early 1970s.

William Nelson, ed., *William Golding's* Lord of the Flies: *A Source Book*. New York: Odyssey Press, 1963. An excellent resource of contemporary reviews and essays on *Lord of the Flies*, including newspaper and periodical reviews as well as theoretical journal articles.

Bernard S. Oldsey and Stanley Weintraub, *The Art of William Golding*. New York: Harcourt Brace and World, 1965. This volume of essays focuses on an examination of the use of fictional perspective in Golding's major novels.

Norman Page, ed., *William Golding: Novels, 1954–1967: A Casebook*. London: Macmillan, 1985. This volume provides a good compilation of criticism on Golding's writing from *Lord of the Flies* to his fiction and essays of the late 1960s.

John Peter, "The Fables of William Golding," *Kenyon Review*, Autumn 1957. Often referred to as the first serious criticism recognizing Golding's book *Lord of the Flies*, this essay addresses the fabulist features of *Lord of the Flies* as well as Golding's second and third novels, *Inheritors* and *Pincher Martin*.

Khandkar Rezaur Rahman, *The Moral Vision of William Golding*. Dhaka, Bangladesh: University of Dhaka, 1990. Developed from the author's Ph.D. dissertation, this volume discusses Golding's works in the context of ethical and theological concerns.

Philip Redpath, *William Golding: A Structural Reading of His Fiction*. Totowa, NJ: Barnes and Noble, 1986. This book of essays subjects Golding's novels to structuralist interpretations. Useful for in-depth scholarship but otherwise too esoteric for young readers.

Patrick Reilly, "*Lord of the Flies:* Beelzebub's Boys." In *The Literature of Guilt: From "Gulliver" to Golding*. Iowa City: University of Iowa Press, 1988. This essay discusses the literary predecessors and origins of *Lord of the Flies* as well as its main characters and themes.

———, Lord of the Flies: *Fathers and Sons*. New York: Twayne, 1992. An excellent volume of essays examining Golding's *Lord of the Flies* in its social and biographical context as well as in the context of other works that influenced Golding, such as Jonathan Swift's *Gulliver's Travels*.

Claire Rosenfield, "'Men of a Smaller Growth': A Psychological Analysis of William Golding's *Lord of the Flies*," *Literature and Psychology*, Autumn 1961. A study proposing *Lord of the Flies* as a psychological novel with roots in the psychoanalytic theories of nineteenth-century psychiatrist Sigmund Freud.

Paul Slayton, "Teaching Rationale for William Golding's *Lord of the Flies*." In Nicholas J. Karolides, Lee Burress, John M. Kean, eds, *Censored Books: Critical Viewpoints*. Lanham, MD: Scarecrow Press, 1993. In this article, Slayton finds *Lord of the Flies* to be a parable about modern civilization and human morality, and describes Golding's literary techniques.

David Spitz, "Power and Authority: An Interpretation of Golding's *Lord of the Flies*," *Antioch Review*, Spring 1970. An analysis of the power dynamics of *Lord of the Flies* suggesting that the novel may be read as a political allegory.

V.V. Subbarao, *William Golding: A Study*. New York: Envoy Press, 1987. This volume of essays, based on the author's Ph.D. dissertation, covers all of Golding's novels through *The Paper Men*.

Henri Talon, "Irony in *Lord of the Flies*," *Essays in Criticism*, July 1968. An analysis of *Lord of the Flies* focusing on the ironic elements of the plot and characters.

John S. Whitley, *Golding:* Lord of the Flies. London: Edward Arnold, 1971. This book contains an introductory essay by the author providing biographical and historical information about *Lord of the Flies* and an essay providing a detailed scene-by-scene reading of the text discussing major themes and critical concerns.

James Wood, "Religious Insights of a Man Apart," *Manchester Guardian Weekly*, September 29, 1991. An excerpt from an essay written as a tribute to Golding on his seventy-fifth birthday in which the author describes his interview with Golding and comments on the principal characteristics of his works.

Historical Background

Jonathan W. Doering, "The Fluctuations of William Golding's Critical Reputation," *Contemporary Review*, May 2002. An essay eulogizing and analyzing the falling in and out of favor of William Golding's literary work.

Herbert N. Foerstel, *Banned in the U.S.A.: A Reference Guide to Book Censorship in Schools and Public Libraries*. Westport, CT: Greenwood Press, 2002. This guide is a useful source of information about historic and contemporary book-banning movements and occurrences.

David Halberstam, *The Fifties*. New York: Balantine Books, 1994. A comprehensive historical and cultural guide to the 1950s in America.

Pat Rogers, *An Outline of English Literature*. New York: Oxford University Press, 1992. This guide provides historical context for trends, movements, and figures in English literature.

Thomas R. Whissen, *Classic Cult Fiction: A Companion to Popular Cult Literature*. New York: Greenwood Press, 1992. A guide to popular novels that have developed impassioned followings since their publications.

Index

Picture Credits

About the Author

Andy Koopmans is the author of several books, including biographies of Bruce Lee, Madonna, and Charles A. Lindbergh. He lives in Seattle, Washington, with his wife, Angela Mihm, their cats, Bubz and Licorice, and their dog, Zachary.

Koopmans wishes to thank William Golding's daughter, Judith Golding Carver, for her invaluable assistance with the biographical portion of this book. Additionally, he would like to thank Jennifer Skancke for assistance in preparing this manuscript for publication.